PEOPLE OF THE LAKES

TIME® LIFE BOOKS

Other Publications:

THE NEW HOME REPAIR AND IMPROVEMENT
JOURNEY THROUGH THE MIND AND BODY
WEIGHT WATCHERS® SMART CHOICE RECIPE COLLECTION
TRUE CRIME
THE ART OF WOODWORKING
LOST CIVILIZATIONS
ECHOES OF GLORY
THE NEW FACE OF WAR
HOW THINGS WORK
WINGS OF WAR
CREATIVE EVERYDAY COOKING
COLLECTOR'S LIBRARY OF THE UNKNOWN
CLASSICS OF WORLD WAR II
TIME-LIFE LIBRARY OF CURIOUS AND UNUSUAL FACTS
AMERICAN COUNTRY
VOYAGE THROUGH THE UNIVERSE
THE THIRD REICH
THE TIME-LIFE GARDENER'S GUIDE
MYSTERIES OF THE UNKNOWN
TIME FRAME
FIX IT YOURSELF
FITNESS, HEALTH & NUTRITION
SUCCESSFUL PARENTING
HEALTHY HOME COOKING
UNDERSTANDING COMPUTERS
LIBRARY OF NATIONS
THE ENCHANTED WORLD
THE KODAK LIBRARY OF CREATIVE PHOTOGRAPHY
GREAT MEALS IN MINUTES
THE CIVIL WAR
PLANET EARTH
COLLECTOR'S LIBRARY OF THE CIVIL WAR
THE EPIC OF FLIGHT
THE GOOD COOK
WORLD WAR II
THE OLD WEST

For information on and a full description of any of the Time-Life
Books series listed above, please call 1-800-621-7026 or write:
Reader Information
Time-Life Customer Service
P.O. Box C-32068
Richmond, Virginia 23261-2068

This volume is one of a series that chronicles the history and culture of the Native Americans. Other books in the series include:

THE FIRST AMERICANS
THE SPIRIT WORLD
THE EUROPEAN CHALLENGE
PEOPLE OF THE DESERT
THE WAY OF THE WARRIOR
THE BUFFALO HUNTERS
REALM OF THE IROQUOIS

THE MIGHTY CHIEFTAINS
KEEPERS OF THE TOTEM
CYCLES OF LIFE
WAR FOR THE PLAINS
TRIBES OF THE SOUTHERN WOODLANDS
THE INDIANS OF CALIFORNIA
PEOPLE OF THE ICE AND SNOW

The Cover: Holding a traditional war club and tobacco
pipe, an Ojibwa man proudly sits for a portrait in a
19th-century photographic studio. His fine clothing
displays masterful examples of glass beadwork, embroidery, and appliqué, European techniques the Great
Lakes Indians learned from Catholic missionaries.

THE AMERICAN INDIANS

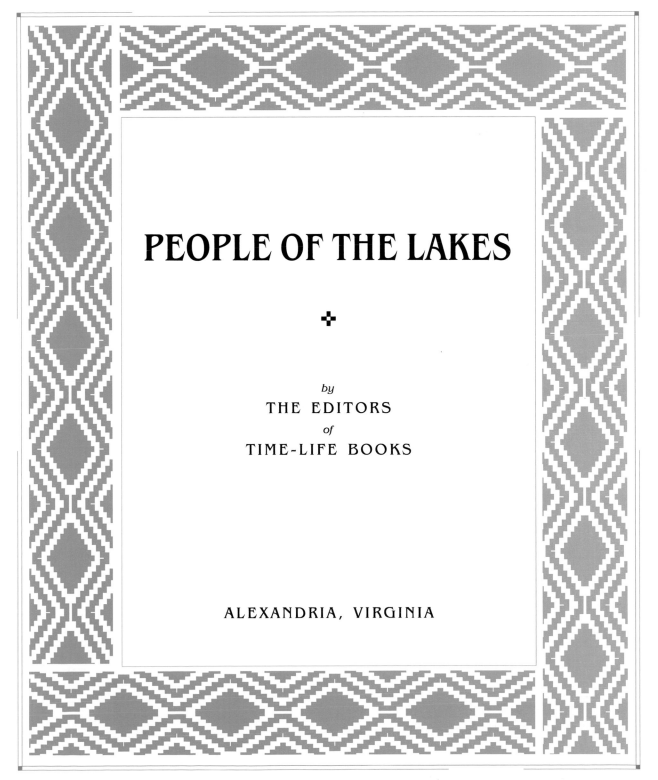

PEOPLE OF THE LAKES

✦

by
THE EDITORS
of
TIME-LIFE BOOKS

ALEXANDRIA, VIRGINIA

THE AMERICAN INDIANS

SERIES EDITOR: Henry Woodhead
Administrative Editor: Loretta Y. Britten

Editorial Staff for *People of the Lakes*
Senior Art Director: Mary Gasperetti
Picture Editor: Jane Coughran
Text Editor: Stephen G. Hyslop
Associate Editors/Research-Writing: Robert H. Wooldridge Jr. (principal), Michael E. Howard, Karen Monks
Senior Copyeditor: Ann Lee Bruen
Picture Coordinator: David Beard
Editorial Assistant: Gemma Villanueva

Special Contributors: Amy Aldrich, Thomas J. Craughwell, George G. Daniels, Maggie Debelius, Marfé Ferguson Delano, Thomas Lewis, David S. Thomson, Gerald P. Tyson (text); Martha Lee Beckington, Jennifer Veech (research); Barbara L. Klein (index).

Correspondents: Elisabeth Kraemer-Singh (Bonn), Christine Hinze (London), Christina Lieberman (New York), Maria Vincenza Aloisi (Paris), Ann Natanson (Rome). Valuable assistance was also provided by: Barbara Gevene Hertz (Copenhagen), Elizabeth Brown, Daniel Donnelly (New York).

Library of Congress Cataloging in Publication Data
People of the lakes/by the editors of Time-Life Books.
   p. cm.—(The American Indians)
Includes bibliographical references and index.
ISBN 0-8094-9566-X
1. Indians of North America—Great Lakes Region—History. 2. Indians of North America—Great Lakes Region—Social life and customs. I. Time-Life Books. II. Series.
E78.G7P43 1994   94-28494
977'.00497—dc20   CIP

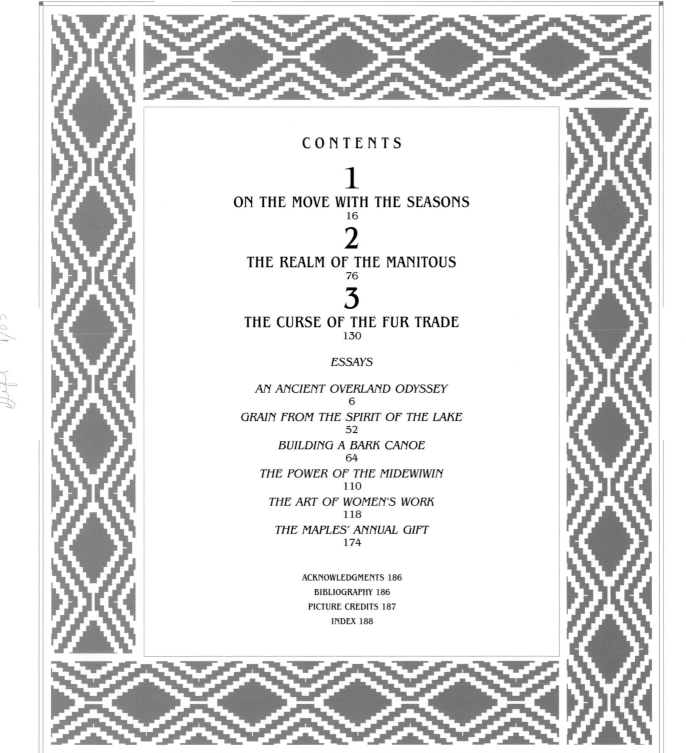

CONTENTS

1
ON THE MOVE WITH THE SEASONS
16

2
THE REALM OF THE MANITOUS
76

3
THE CURSE OF THE FUR TRADE
130

ESSAYS

AN ANCIENT OVERLAND ODYSSEY

"If you do not move, you will be destroyed," proclaimed a prophet to the Anishinabe, or Original People, the forerunners of the Ojibwa and other Algonquian-speaking tribes of the Great Lakes region. According to legend, the Anishinabe heeded the words of that prophet, who may have been warning of the arrival of the white man. They left their villages by the great salt sea on the east coast of North America and embarked on an epic westward journey in search of a new homeland, "where food grows on the water."

The people of the lakes have long celebrated that ancestral migration in songs, stories, and pictographs inscribed on birch-bark scrolls by members of a sacred society called the Midewiwin. Some say the Anishinabe reached the lakes region by venturing up the Saint Lawrence River past Niagara Falls—the route traced below *(arrows)* and illustrated on the following pages. Others maintain that the travelers left the Saint Lawrence at midcourse and headed up the Ottawa River *(dotted line)* before turning westward. But all agree that the Anishinabe were guided by signs from the spirits that led them to a bountiful country, where sustenance in the form of wild rice emerged from the water as promised.

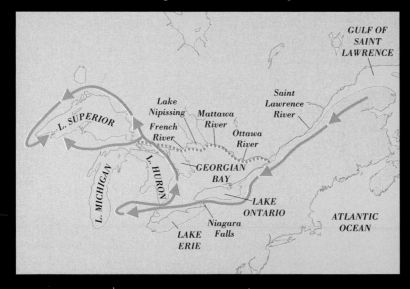

The sun rises over the Atlantic near the mouth of the Saint Lawrence, where the Anishinabe began their journey, recounted on birch-bark scrolls like the one at right. Portrayed there are sacred beings, including the otter and turtle, shown at either end of a body of water that may be Lake Superior.

In the first stage of a migration that continued for generations, the Anishinabe moved southwestward up the Saint Lawrence River (left) until they reached the Place of the Thunder Water, or Niagara Falls (below).

In time, the Anishi-
nabe reached the
area around Lake
Huron and Georgian
Bay, dotted by hun-
dreds of rocky is-
lands (below). The
region abounded
with stands of birch-
es (left), whose bark
served many pur-
poses for the Origi-
nal People, from ca-
noe building to
recordkeeping.

After crossing from island to island and reaching the north end of Lake Huron, the Anishinabe divided at the rapids they called Bawating (Sault Sainte Marie) and proceeded around the north and south shores of Lake Superior, where they came upon places of power and beauty that remain sacred to their descendants. At left, an ancient cedar twists skyward on the north shore of Lake Superior. Above, a waterfall plunges off a rocky cliff on the south shore.

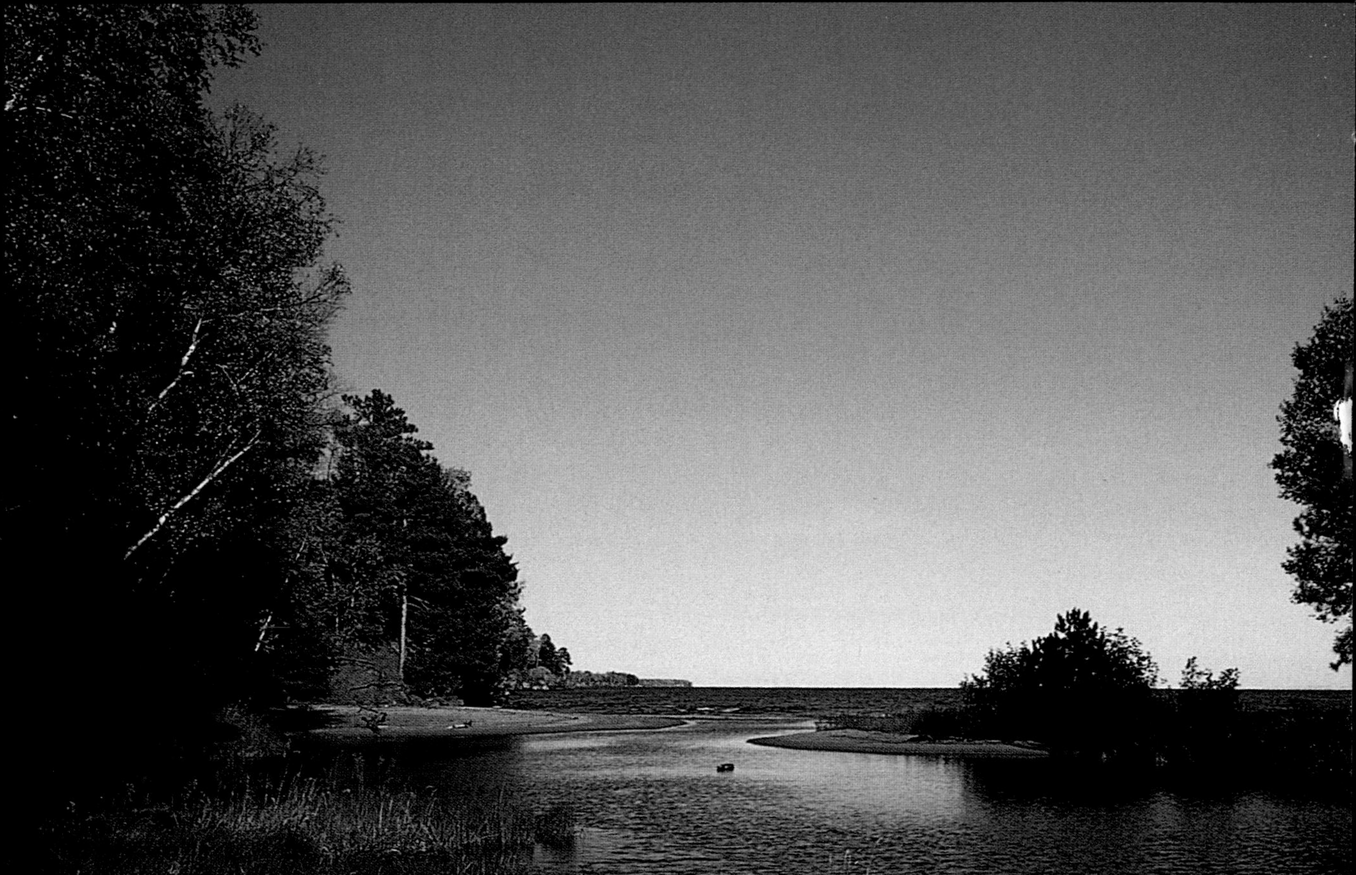

The long journey of the Anishinabe brought them here to Madeline Island, near the western end of Lake Superior. Tribal history attests that the spirits who had guided the ancestors from the great salt sea sent a sign in the form of a sacred shell, which rose from the water to show the people that this was their appointed destination.

1

An Ojibwa family, equipped with a rifle and snowshoes, stands outside its wigwam at a winter hunting camp. An Indian invention, the snowshoe (inset) typically consisted of rawhide netting stretched on a rounded ash frame; the Menominee called this particular design a "catfish" because of its shape.

ON THE MOVE WITH THE SEASONS

Winter came early to the people of the lakes. By late September—a time known to the Ojibwa as the Shining Leaf Moon—the birches were turning golden, and the sugar maples were touched with crimson. By October, or the Falling Leaf Moon, chill winds were sweeping down from the northwest, combing the leaves from the branches and raising whitecaps on the blue water. By November, or the Freezing Moon, snow blanketed the forest trails, and woodland creatures were making ready for the long, cold siege that lay ahead. Beavers settled into their lodges, and black bears repaired to their dens.

In their villages, however, it was time for families to count their blessings and move on. The food they had set by during the short growing season—corn and squash from their gardens, berries from the meadows, wild rice from the marshes—would eventually be exhausted in the absence of fresh provisions. To survive the harsh winter, the villagers would have to divide into small groups and set out for hunting camps, where the men would stalk deer and other game and spear or net fish beneath the ice.

The people planned for this move far in advance, marking the time on calendars of their own devising. "My father kept count of the days on a stick," recalled an Ojibwa woman named Nodinens, who grew up in the Mille Lacs region of central Minnesota in the mid-1800s, when many of her people were still pursuing the strenuous seasonal round of their ancestors. "He had a stick long enough to last a year," she added, "and he always began a new stick in the fall. He cut a big notch for the first day of a new moon and a small notch for each of the other days."

With every notch her father made on the stick during the fall, Nodinens and her mother and grandmother stepped up their efforts to prepare their household for the impending move. Using bone needles and cord stripped from boiled basswood bark, they wove portable mats of bulrushes to cover the pole framework of their winter wigwam. And as the days grew colder, they stockpiled lightweight bundles of food—wild rice, berries, and seasonings such as dried pumpkin flowers. By the time ice

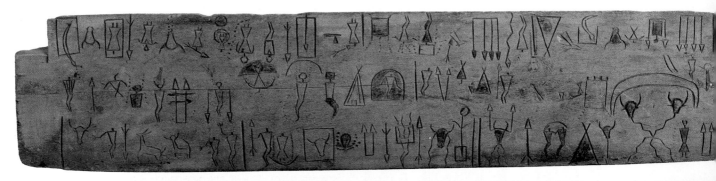

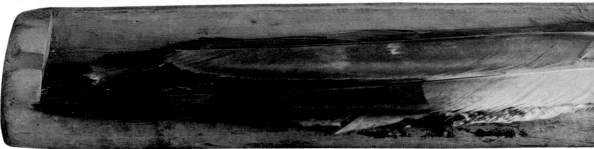

formed on the lakes, they were ready to travel. They rolled the mats up tightly around their blankets to form handy bundles. When Nodinens's mother still had an infant to care for, she wedged the baby snugly inside the bundle, cradleboard and all.

The cover of a wooden box containing an eagle-feather headdress features a pictographic record of a sacred Ojibwa song. Similar symbols were drawn on birch bark to record the Ojibwa's ancient Midewiwin texts.

Five other families accompanied Nodinens and her family on their annual trek. "When we found a nice place in the deep woods, we made our winter camp," she related. "The men shoveled away the snow in a big space, and the six wigwams were put in a circle and banked with evergreen boughs and snow. Of course, the snow was all shoveled away inside of the wigwam, and plenty of cedar boughs were spread on the ground and covered with blankets for our beds." A fire burned at the center of the camp as well as at the center of each wigwam: "We always slept barefoot, with our feet toward the fire," remembered Nodinens.

By limiting their winter camp to several families, the Ojibwa guarded against the possibility of depleting the limited game in any one area—a danger that was all the greater after Ojibwa hunters carried guns in place of their traditional bows and arrows. Each day, the men ventured out, wearing snowshoes when the drifts were deep, and more often than not, they returned with their hands full. "My father was a good hunter and sometimes killed two deer in a day," Nodinens recalled. "Some hunters

took a sled to bring back the game, but more frequently they brought back only part of the animal, and the women went next day and packed the rest of the meat on their backs. It was the custom for a man to give a feast with the first deer or other game that he killed. The deer was cut up, boiled, and seasoned nicely, and all the other families were invited to the feast. Each family gave such a feast when the man killed his first game."

Most of the time, the skill and generosity of the hunters kept all the families well provided for. But on one occasion, their good fortune was dispelled by an evil omen. A hunter was returning to camp one day when he heard an owl following him. "You must preserve every bit of deer," he told the women back at the camp. "This is a bad sign, and we will not get any more game." Sure enough, luck abandoned the hunters, and their rations ran short. "We were so hungry that we had to dig roots and boil them," Nodinens recollected.

Fortunately, her father belonged to the Midewiwin—a medicine society whose members knew how to counter evil influences. The young man who was serving as leader of the camp knew of her father's powers and approached him with gifts of berries, tobacco, and a kettle of rice. "Our friend," the young man implored him, "we are in danger of starving; help us." Eager to oblige, Nodinens's father called together others of his society in the camp. "The men sang Mide songs and shook their rattles," his daughter related. "The children were put to bed early and told that they must not even look up. My mother sat up and kept the fire burning." Later that evening, Nodinens's father returned to the family wigwam and sang a sacred song. Just then, a mysterious voice was heard outside the lodge, joining in the song: "It was a woman's voice, and my mother heard it plainly. This was considered a good omen."

Filled with hope, Nodinens's father rose the following morning and directed that a fire be kindled some distance from the camp. There he and his fellow Midewiwin gathered to sing once more: "They put sweet grass and medicine on the fire and let the smoke cover their bodies, their clothing, and their guns. When this was finished, my father covered his hand with red paint and applied it to the shoulders of the men. They took their guns and started to hunt, feeling sure that they would succeed." Before long they and their families were feasting gratefully on the flesh of animals that had long eluded them.

"After that," Nodinens remembered with pride, "whenever we were short of game, they brought a kettle of rice to my father, and he sang, and the luck would return."

Through dedication and persistence, the people of the lakes have long managed to endure in one of North America's more stringent environments—a rugged land that was sculpted ages ago by glacial action and that still reverts to a wintry, icy state for nearly six months out of the year. The Great Lakes, and the thousands of smaller lakes around them, formed at the end of the last Ice Age as the heavy glaciers melted and receded northward, leaving behind depressions in the landscape and copious reserves of water to fill them. The emergent lakes were at first surrounded by marshy tundra, which provided good grazing for mammoths and mastodons and smaller herbivores such as caribou. The plentiful game in turn lured the first humans to the region—hunters whose ancestors had crossed overland from Siberia during the Ice Age.

A Huron couple from Quebec exhibit a mixture of European and traditional clothing in this 18th-century watercolor by an unknown artist.

Gradually, this hunting ground was transformed. As the climate warmed, the tundra gave way to a forest of cedar and pine interspersed with birch, maple, oak, and other deciduous trees. For the hunting bands that settled around the lakes, there was fresh quarry to be taken. The giant herbivores were extinct and the caribou had retreated northward, but the woodlands teemed with ample substitutes, including deer, bear, moose—and in the grassy clearings at the southern and western fringes of the lakes region, bison.

The land offered other rewards to its early occupants. From the beginning, fish were a vital resource for the people of the lakes. And eventually, the gather-

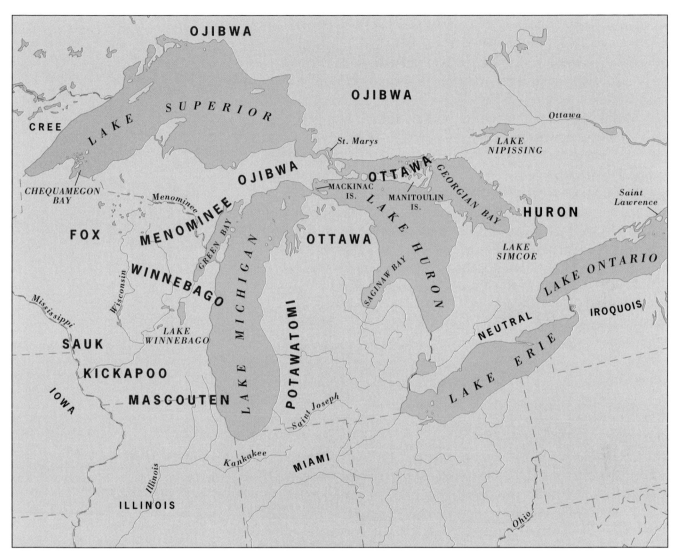

When Europeans arrived in the Great Lakes region in the 1600s, they found several related tribes living there: The Ottawa settled on Manitoulin Island and a finger of land between Lake Huron and Georgian Bay as well as on the northern tip of the peninsula between Lakes Michigan and Huron; the Potawatomi camped near the southeastern shores of Lake Michigan; and the Ojibwa dwelt around Lake Superior. Neighbors, including the Sauk, Menominee, and Fox, shared the region's abundant resources.

ing of wild seeds and grasses was augmented in places by the planting of beans, squash, and corn, all of which were introduced to the lakes region before AD 1000. Agriculture had a major impact on tribes living at the lower end of the Great Lakes, where the growing season stretched to four months or more and the harvests were substantial. In the colder central zone, however, corn and other crops remained mere supplements to the traditional diet. Farther north, above Lake Superior, the summer was too brief and the soil too poor for cultivation, and native peoples subsisted as their ancestors had, by hunting, fishing, and gathering nuts and berries.

Although the precise movements of the region's tribes cannot be reconstructed with certainty before they came in contact with Europeans in the early 1600s, there were unsettling developments in the northern woodlands prior to that time. Beginning in the 1500s, encounters between Europeans and Indians who were living along the Atlantic coast and the Gulf of Saint Lawrence gradually spread disease and disruption inland. And well before that, intertribal conflict was evidently on the increase in the woodlands, perhaps because surpluses of dried corn provided portable food for warriors on far-ranging expeditions. Bitter feuds broke out between rival groups in the woodlands long before the Iroquois living in present-day New York State acquired firearms in trade from the Dutch and the English and launched long-distance raids that drove tribes temporarily from their homelands around the Great Lakes. Amid such strife and uncertainty, some of the bands probably were displaced or chose to abandon their territories for more promising sites.

Several tribes of the lakes region have preserved legends of an ancient migration. The Ojibwa—sometimes referred to as the Chippewa—tell of an epic journey that long ago brought their ancestors to the shores of Lake Superior from the east. In the beginning, the story goes, their ancestors lived in the land of the rising sun, near the great salt sea that whites would call the Atlantic. For generations, the people had prospered there, drawing on the bounty of the eastern forests and lakes. They called themselves the Anishinabe, or Original People. In those early years, one version of the legend says, the Original People "were so many and powerful that if one was to climb the highest mountain and look in all directions, he would not be able to see the end of the nation." Living in small bands, the Anishinabe were scattered across a broad area. But they kept in contact, traveling by canoe and overland trail to exchange goods and hold councils.

Then came a warning from a prophet. "If you do not move," he told the people, "you will be destroyed." The prophet urged them to seek out an island in the shape of a turtle. That would be their first stopping point. There would be six more, and each one would be revealed through a sacred sign—the Megis—a cowrie shell that first emerged from the great salt sea. Many among the Anishinabe were skeptical, reluctant to leave a land of plenty. Then, one night, a pregnant woman had a prophetic dream in which she saw herself standing on a turtle, with its head pointed toward the land of the setting sun. The turtle lay in a river that flowed westward. When the elders learned of this dream, they pressed the Anishinabe to leave the coast and search for the visionary island in the direction of the setting sun. Not all the people heeded them, however. One brave band, known as the Daybreak People, believed that the prophecy would come to pass but stayed by the salt sea in order to guard the eastern doorway to the continent for the Anishinabe and to tend the eastern fire. According to legend, they and others who remained near the ocean were eventually destroyed by a light-skinned race.

For many years, the Anishinabe journeyed westward, mostly by canoe. Some say they paddled up the Saint Lawrence River and found the turtle-shaped mound not far from present-day Montreal, where a small island sits at the mouth of a westward-flowing river called the Saint Francis. After dwelling there for a while, the Anishinabe heeded the words of the prophet and continued their migration, seeking the sacred sign that would assure them they were on the right course. In time, the Megis appeared to the people at the Place of the Thunder Water, or Niagara Falls, where they beheld it rising from the foam. Thereafter, the Megis appeared to them out of the water, for while the Anishinabe had left the ocean behind, they remained tied by destiny to majestic lakes and rushing rivers.

During their great journey, which lasted many generations, the Anishinabe encountered enemies and subdued them, profiting by their strength in numbers. At night, it was said, their campfires flickered "like stars for as far as the eye could see." All the campfires were kindled from one sacred fire, which had been carried from the land of the rising sun and was never allowed to die.

As the long trek continued, legend has it, the Anishinabe divided into three groups and went their separate ways, with each group assuming a different responsibility for sustaining the culture. One pledged to safeguard the sacred fire. These people became known as the Potawatomi. Another group agreed to carry out major trading expeditions. These became the Ottawa. The third group was to protect the spiritual beliefs of the Anishinabe and emerged as the Ojibwa. From their ranks would come the Midewiwin, who would preserve the sacred lore of the people in words, in songs, and in the symbols they inscribed on their unique birch-bark scrolls.

The trader people, or Ottawa, found homes on Manitoulin Island at the northern end of Lake Huron and on the mainland nearby. It was there, in what is today the Canadian province of Ontario, that Europeans first came upon their

An 18th-century portrait shows the upswept hair style and body painting of the Ottawa. Before the introduction of trade cloth, most Ottawa men covered themselves with tattoos rather than elaborate clothing.

villages. In 1615 the French explorer Samuel de Champlain encountered a large group of Ottawas near the mouth of the French River, due east of Manitoulin Island. Struck by the way in which the men coaxed their hair into a sort of elevated ridge, he dubbed them *cheveux relevés*, or "raised hairs." Others who dealt with them early on observed that Ottawa men wore their hair high in front but short in the back, which purportedly gave pursuing enemies less to take hold of. So energetic were they at trade, Champlain noted, that some of their parties would journey several hundred miles or more to exchange goods with other tribes.

The Potawatomi, for their part, settled in the southwestern part of present-day Michigan, where fish and game were abundant and where the climate and soil were conducive to farming. Agriculture provided them some security, but they still dispersed to hunting grounds in the late fall to make it through the winter. In the spring, some parties would venture south to stalk bison on the patches of prairie that emerged from the woodlands below the lakes. Although the Potawatomi were not unique among tribes of the region for their hospitality and diplomacy, they did justice to their reputation as keepers of the sacred fire by bringing rival groups together to arbitrate disputes and by lavishing food and other bounty on their guests. One French visitor to a Potawatomi village in the 1600s was entertained royally with a feast that included boiled whitefish, the tongue and breast of a deer, beaver's tail, bear's feet, a pair of wood hens, a savory stew, and a sweet beverage of water mixed with maple syrup.

The Ojibwa, meanwhile, had settled farther to the north, along Lake Superior. As guardians of the spiritual traditions of the Anishinabe, it was said, they continued to be guided by the Megis after parting from the others. In time, that sacred sign appeared to them at another place of beauty and bounty—the strait where waters from Lake Superior rushed down to the lower-lying Lake Huron. There, where whitefish choked the rapids, the Ojibwa paused and established a village they called Bawating, or Place at the Falls. Some of the Ojibwas remained in the area, while others eventually continued on around Lake Superior.

Bawating was not only a splendid fishery but also a hub for waterborne trade. French explorers and traders who arrived there in the 17th century dubbed the local Indians Saulteurs, an adaptation of the French word *saut,* or "falls." The place became known to the French as Sault Sainte Marie. Frenchman Claude de La Potherie, writing about 1700, marveled at the skill with which Saulteurs negotiated the rapids in their canoes to snare the swarming whitefish: "They cast their nets headlong into

Ojibwa men use long-handled nets to snare whitefish in the rapids at Sault Sainte Marie, Ontario, about 1900. Their fishing techniques are similar to those recorded more than 200 years earlier in a drawing (inset) by French artist Louis Nicolas.

Hail Storm, an Ontario Ojibwa, donned native dress for an 1843 tour of England. British audiences, including novelist Charles Dickens, flocked to see the Ojibwas in traditional costumes and jewelry, including pieces like this incised silver bracelet (inset).

the boiling waters," he wrote.

"The tumult of the waters in which they are floating seems to them only a diversion; they see in it the fish, heaped up on one another, that are endeavoring to force their way through the rapids; and when they feel their nets heavy, they draw them in." The village had a permanent population of several hundred people, a number that swelled to two or three thousand each summer as Ojibwas and others from the surrounding area congregated there to fish, trade, hold diplomatic councils, and join in ceremonies.

By the time Frenchmen reached Bawating, many Ojibwas were fanning out around Lake Superior. According to legend, those who ventured to the western end of that lake were again blessed with a vision of the Megis. That sign appeared to the people for the last time at La Pointe Island—or Madeline Island, as it is known today—where Ojibwas founded a bustling village that emerged as the spiritual center of their culture. There at La Pointe, one Ojibwa later remarked, the Mide rites were practiced in

Tiered earrings and expensive clothing indicate the high status of Mas-saw, a prominent Potawatomi. Her blouse resembles one with brooches of German silver (inset), an alloy made of nickel, zinc, and copper.

their "purest and most original form."

Even though the Ojibwa, Ottawa, and Potawatomi occupied distinct territories, they spoke related Algonquian languages and acknowledged their common traditions by referring to themselves as the Three Fires. They were linked by language and custom to several other tribes living around Lakes Superior, Michigan, and Huron when Europeans arrived. Among the other Algonquian speakers of the western Great Lakes were the Menominee, Kickapoo, Sauk, and Fox, also known as the Mesquakie, all of whom were first encountered by whites in the vicinity of present-day Wisconsin; and the Miami and Illinois, whose ancestral territory lay below Lake Michigan. With the Three Fires, these tribes have been labeled the central Algonquians, to distinguish them from the eastern Algonquians along the Atlantic coast. The peripheries of the lakes were home to tribes belonging to

two other language groups—to
the west, the Siouan-speaking Winnebago of lower Wisconsin and, to the
east, the Iroquoian-speaking Huron at the southern end of Georgian Bay.

When Champlain initially came upon the Huron in the early 1600s,
they were trading amicably with various Algonquian tribes, while at the
same time feuding bitterly with the Five Nations of the Iroquois confeder-
acy to their south. In the mid-1600s, the Huron homeland was overrun by
the Iroquois. Some surviving Hurons fled westward and sought refuge
among central Algonquian peoples, who would soon face sharp challenges of their own from Iroquois war parties.

The escalating conflict between the Iroquois and the people of the
lakes was the result of longstanding animosities, aggravated by competition for the furs that European traders prized. But in many respects, the
customs and traditions of the rival groups were quite similar. Both divided
their communities into clans that claimed descent primarily from animal

Big Sail, an Ottawa chief, wears around his neck what is probably a British peace medal. A similar medallion (inset), inscribed with the name of Ottawa leader Matchiwita, was likely presented by Englishmen eager to control the Great Lakes fur trade in the 1800s.

Grizzly Bear, a Menominee chieftain, carries a sacred calumet. The Menominee believed tobacco had mystical properties, and so they took great care in crafting their pipestems, such as this wooden model carved with a floral design and inlaid with silver (inset).

spirits. And when it came to warfare, both the Iroquois and their opponents around the western Great Lakes practiced similar rituals of retribution. War parties atoned for the loss of loved ones by capturing enemies, who were either adopted by the grieving families or put to death. Captors sometimes ate some of the flesh of the condemned men as a way of claiming their bravery and strength.

Assaults by the Iroquois were not the only shocks sustained by the Indians of the western Great Lakes. By the time the raids reached their peak in the 1650s, many of the region's indigenous peoples had already been depleted by diseases communicated by European intruders. And once the Iroquois threat subsided, further trials lay ahead—wars between rival European powers that proved ruinous for many of the native peoples caught up in them and a rising tide of white settlement. By the mid-19th century, many Indians from the southern part of the region had been forced from their homelands. Some displaced groups ended up in strange and distant

settings. The Sauk and the Fox—
who were so closely allied for a time that they were spoken of as one tribe—were driven westward, ending up on reservations in Iowa and Kansas. A small number of Winnebagos managed to hold out in the woods of Wisconsin, but the rest were relocated repeatedly by federal officials, with the majority ending up in Nebraska. The Kickapoo, for their part, underwent an epic series of displacements that saw part of the tribe driven all the way to Mexico—an odyssey that spanned centuries and rivaled the fabled journey of the Anishinabe.

Black Hawk, the Sauk leader who made a last effort at repelling the whites during the 1832 Black Hawk War, holds a fan made from the feathers of his namesake bird. Contemporary Sauks continue to use feather fans (inset) as part of their ceremonial regalia.

As for those calling themselves the Three Fires, many Ottawas and some Potawatomis managed to retain footholds in their ancestral domain. But it was the Ojibwa of the northern lake country who persisted in their homeland in the greatest numbers. They were fortunate in that their ancestors had occupied a densely forested country that was not easily penetrated by hostile warriors and offered little to attract white farmers.

Wakusasse, a Fox warrior, wears a roach made of deer and porcupine hair. The traditional roach headdress (inset) is attached to a scalp lock to create a crest recalling that of the woodpecker, a bird long associated with war by the Fox.

The Ojibwa had even managed to expand their territory in the 1700s by driving rival Dakota Sioux from the Mille Lacs area and other parts of Minnesota. To be sure, they subsequently faced serious challenges to their independent way of life. The fur trade they had come to rely on dwindled; mining and lumber companies made inroads on their territory; and American and Canadian authorities imposed treaties that reduced the tribe's once-vast domain to several scattered reservations. Nevertheless, the Ojibwa adapted and endured. Many found employment with the timber industry. And when business was slow and work scarce, Ojibwas in both Canada and the United States—like other native peoples who remained in the region—supported themselves as they had in earlier days, by hunting, fishing, and harvesting food from gardens, meadows, and marshes.

Today there are nearly 200,000 people of Ojibwa descent living in the northern lakes country, many of them in urban areas but others in small

communities where some of the
old ways persist. As one of the largest Native American groups north of
Mexico, they have kept alive their own heritage as well as that of related
groups who once prospered in the area but have since been scattered
across the continent. A great deal of what we know today about the age-
old traditions of the people of the Great Lakes region has come to us from
the Ojibwa. Yet they are not alone in honoring the memory of the ancestral Anishinabe. All native groups who trace their descent to the region
and reflect that treasured legacy in their customs and lore are helping to
perpetuate the beliefs and practices of the Original People.

Hoowaunneka, or Little Elk, a Winnebago chief whose portrait was painted during an 1828 trip to Washington, D.C., wears several shell necklaces. The Winnebago liked to make such chokers from shells obtained in trade (inset).

In a sense, the journey of the Anishinabe never ceased. For the people of
the lakes, movement from place to place in search of sustenance became
part of the annual round, although villagers generally confined their seasonal forays to familiar territory and returned to the same site each summer. In the warmer months, they usually traveled by water, taking advan-

The Kickapoo Ahtonwetuk, or the Cock Turkey, prays with a prayer stick carved with symbols to aid his memory. He was a disciple of the Kickapoo prophet Kennekuk, who crafted the maple-wood prayer stick shown above.

tage of the innumerable lakes, rivers, and streams that laced their homeland. Many journeys required portages, or overland treks between navigable waterways, passages that would have been very difficult if the people had relied solely on heavy dugout canoes of the sort made by tribes to the south. In addition to fashioning dugouts, most Indians of the region built lightweight canoes, using the bark of a tree that was among their greatest natural assets—the birch.

Despite its fragile appearance, the pale, papery bark of the birch was tough, flexible, and resistant to damage from water or insects. It served many purposes besides that of canoe building. Birch-bark containers called *makuks* were used for gathering wild fruits and storing food. The bark was also made into mats and panels used for the exterior of homes. So durable were the objects made from birch bark that some fragments have been uncovered more than four centuries after they were made, still showing clearly the awl marks where the panels were sewn together.

Among the Ojibwa, the building of a birch-bark canoe was a consummate talent, one thought to be a gift from the spirits. Only a few men in each community were skilled in the manufacture of such a craft. Although one man was in charge of building a canoe, others participated. Birch bark for the canoes was harvested in the spring, when it had the proper resiliency; bark gathered in the summer had a tendency to bubble and split into thin sheets. Early in the season, men would locate good trees—those used for the skin of a canoe had to have a broad trunk that rose to a considerable height before branching. Once an appropriate tree had been found, a blessing was offered to its spirit. The bark was then removed in one piece, carefully rolled and tied with spruce root, and carried back to camp, where it was submerged in water to keep it soft.

While some men were busy collecting birch bark, others combed the forest for cedar timbers for the canoe's skeleton. Often the men returned to trees they had girdled the year before and felled the dead timber, splitting the trunks with wedges made from bone and stone. The logs were then bundled together and carried back to camp. Meanwhile, the women searched for the long, slender spruce roots that would be used to sew and lash the skin to the frame. From experience, Ojibwa women knew to seek

In 1913 an Ojibwa family makes a voyage in its birch-bark canoe in Ontario. Artist George Catlin, who visited the region in the 1800s, was impressed with the vessels: "They are so ingeniously sewed and shaped together that they ride upon the water as light as a cork."

solitary trees, whose roots would not be entangled with those of others. After grubbing up the roots, the women tapped pine or spruce trees for pitch to seal the seams of the canoe. Collecting enough pitch to seal one canoe might require tapping as many as six trees for several days.

Once all the materials had been assembled, the canoe maker supervised the painstaking process of construction. The result was a watertight vessel capable of safely transporting a family and all its possessions from camp to camp. Most birch-bark canoes built by the people of the lakes weighed less than 60 pounds and drew just a few inches of water. Families guarded their canoes carefully. To protect the vessels—and themselves—they generally kept close to shore, where the waters were calmer, and avoided venturing out in stormy weather. They also took care to propitiate the spirits believed to lurk in the depths. Before crossing a bay, the paddlers might scatter tobacco on the water's surface to appease the water monster thought to lie in wait to trap and drown unwary paddlers.

Gathering materials for canoe building was just one of many vital activities that absorbed the people of the lakes in springtime. In late March or early April, when the sap began to swell in the trees, they packed their belongings and moved from their winter hunting camps to maple-sugaring grounds. Maple sugar was their principal seasoning. It was also eaten plain or mixed with water to drink. Each small group of families had its own stand of maple trees—or sugarbush, as it was known. There, cedar spikes, birch-bark buckets, and other equipment used to tap the trees were stored year round in lodges, where the sap drawn each spring was then boiled down.

Like native peoples elsewhere, the tribes of the region gave thanks to the spirits for the earth's gifts. Thus, the first sugar that crystallized from the boiled syrup each season was honored with ceremony and prayer. This ceremonial sugar was traditionally prepared in separate containers. When it was ready, the cluster of families held a feast in its honor. The host spoke quietly to the spirits, asking for good health, safety, and long life for all present. Then each person tasted a small amount of the sugar; an offering of maple sugar might be carried to nearby graves as well. Afterward the guests dined heartily. Later there were dances and games such as dice.

Families remained in their maple sugar camps for several weeks, until the sap stopped flowing. While the women were busy with the trees and boiling troughs, the men ventured from camp to fish in nearby lakes and

streams. Frequently, a thick layer of ice still remained on the water, and the men had to cut through it to reach the fish. After piercing the ice, the fisherman would lie flat over the hole with his head and shoulders covered with a blanket or robe. This veil blocked the sunlight and made it easier for him to spot his prey. Often he dangled a wooden lure into the water, holding his spear poised to thrust. When a fish came into view, he swiftly plunged his weapon home.

Fishing was a year-round activity for the people of the lakes, but the spring fishing run, which followed sugaring season, was urgent because it came at a time of general scarcity. When the ice cleared, the sturgeon left the Great Lakes and surged up the rivers to spawn. Unlike salmon, most sturgeon lived on after spawning, and it was the native custom to snare them on their return journey to the lake. "In order to catch them, the Indians constructed a framework across the river," a 19th-century observer

In camp during the early spring at Mille Lacs, Minnesota, an Ojibwa family boils down sap to make maple sugar. A prosperous woman might own more than 1,000 birch-bark vessels (right) for gathering sap, all of which would be used continuously during maple-sugaring season.

recalled. "This was made by sinking heavy poles like piling not far apart. On top of these they placed timbers strong enough for persons to sit upon, and between the poles they strung basswood cord back and forth until it formed a stout netting through which the fish could not pass. When the fish came down the river, the Indians, seated on the framework, caught them with hooks and killed them with clubs."

The rest of the year, the people went after whitefish, pickerel, and a host of other species. The French officer Antoine de la Mothe Cadillac, who spent considerable time among the Ottawa and other tribes of the region in the late 17th century, referred to fish as a "daily manna, which never fails." Better fish could not be found, he added, for "they are bathed and nourished in the purest water, the clearest and most pellucid you could see anywhere." Netting was the most common and effective fishing technique, and was used both by men and by women, who wove the nets from various fibers. In shallow waters, they laid their seines in the water each night, attached to stakes, and pulled in a healthy catch the next morning. To attract fish, the net might be sprinkled with the powdered roots of certain plants believed to appeal to the creatures. Before being used again, nets were washed thoroughly and rinsed with a preparation of sumac leaves to kill any lingering fish odor that might frighten away future quarry. Indians sometimes lured fish at night with the light of torches made of twisted birch bark or some other material, steeped in pitch. The technique so impressed early French visitors to northern Wisconsin that they dubbed several places there Lac du Flambeau, or Torch Lake.

There were various ways of preparing fish. Part of the catch might be roasted or boiled for immediate consumption. Cadillac retained a powerful impression of a stew the Indians of the region called *sagamity,* which consisted of whitefish boiled in a mixture of water and cornmeal. "This is not dainty food," he remarked, "but it is certainly very wholesome, for it always keeps the bowels open." Much of the catch was preserved for future consumption, however. In colder weather, fish were frozen whole—they were thought to keep longer if they had not been cleaned. During the warmer months, the catch was dried, either in the sun or over a fire. One technique was to dry it completely and pack the fish away. Another was to dry the catch partially, then remove the skin and bones and lay the flesh on a sheet of birch bark, where it completed the drying process. The desiccated fillets were then rubbed between the hands until soft and fine, mixed with maple sugar, and packed in birch-bark containers for storage. The mixture was considered a special delicacy.

With the end of the spring fishing run came yet another move. In the last days of May, those groups who planted crops moved to their summer villages. There they tended their gardens, gathered wild fruits and herbs as they came into season, and engaged in various warm-weather crafts. Nodinens of the Mille Lacs Ojibwa recalled how the six families of her winter camp moved together to the maple-sugaring ground and then returned to their home village in late spring. Each family there "had a large bark house, with a platform along each side," she noted. Some bark-covered houses had peaked roofs and were preferred over wigwams as summer dwellings because the heat rose up into the roof. In addition to such peaked lodges and the dome-shaped wigwams, tipis, covered with the same materials as their other dwellings, were sometimes erected at camps. The Mille Lacs villagers left their bark houses standing through the year. "We renewed the bark if necessary," Nodinens recollected, "and this was our summer home." Every family also had its own garden nearby, she added, and the men would till the soil "with old axes, bones, or anything that would cut and break up the ground. My father had wooden hoes that he made, and sometimes we used the shoulder blade of a large deer or a moose, holding it in the hand."

Once the soil was tilled, the women planted seeds—traditionally, corn, beans, and squash—in rows of hillocks. After the sowing was done, a shaman, or spiritual leader, prepared a feast at which people appealed to the spirits for a bountiful harvest. While they waited for their crops to ripen, villagers fished, hunted, and gathered. Berry picking was largely done by women and children—although, among the Winnebago, men participated as well. After strapping their makuks to their waists, the harvesters set to the task, plucking blueberries, gooseberries, raspberries, or other delicacies. At first, the hungry villagers gorged on the sweet harvest. Later, large amounts were preserved. Blueberries and other types of fruit were dried whole on reed frames—with four makuks of fresh berries providing about one makuk of dried fruit. Raspberries were often cooked to a paste, then spread over sheets of birch bark in small, thin cakes, which were laid out in the sun until the moisture evaporated. The dried cakes were then stacked and tied in bundles for storage.

Much of what the women harvested from their gardens was also preserved. They dried the corn and either stored it whole or knocked free the kernels and ground them into meal. Squash was sliced into round pieces and smoked or dried in the sun. Traditionally, the tribes of the region stored surplus crops in underground caches lined with birch bark. Wood-

Menominees fishing at night use iron fire baskets to attract fish to the surface in this 1845 painting by Paul Kane. Today's Ojibwas continue this ancient practice, wearing miner's hard hats with halogen lamps to lure the fish within range of their spears.

en beams were laid over the cache, and it was covered with a mound of earth. Part of the harvest, of course, was steamed, roasted, or boiled and eaten fresh. The Winnebago followed an elaborate steaming process to cook large quantities of dried corn. First they pounded the ears on a rack to separate the kernels from the cob. Then they placed the grain in a pit, atop red-hot stones lined with husks. Finally, they laid another layer of husks on top of the kernels, poured water in, sealed the pit with earth, and left the corn to cook overnight.

During the summer months, the women were also busy gathering and processing wild plants from the woods and meadows. One of the most important items they culled was the inner bark of the basswood tree, a soft yellow fiber that was cut into strips and used for a variety of purposes. The thickest bands of basswood bark were interwoven to form baskets or containers for boiling resin from trees. The finest strands were fashioned into twine for sewing together mats, among other purposes. Another useful fiber was derived from the wood nettle. The stalks were allowed to dry in the field before being harvested; then they were soaked for about 10 days so that the fibers could be easily removed and twined together by hand to form a strong cord. Cloth was sometimes woven from fine nettle-fiber cord, while a coarser twine was used to make animal traps and fishnets. Knotting the twine into mesh was a painstaking job: Nevertheless, some Ojibwa fishnets measured more than 200 feet in length.

The summer months were also the time for collecting bulrushes and cattails, which were stitched together with sturdy twine to form floor mats or wall coverings. Large quantities of stalks were collected, dried, and boiled. Some of them were tinted using vegetable dyes. In the weaving process, performed on a wooden frame or loom, these colored stalks were used to create patterns—stripes, lattices, and diamonds. While weaving rush mats, women were careful to keep the stalks moist; otherwise they might break in the middle of a row, ruining the mat. Women wove rushes only in the morning or evening, when the sun was not too hot. Whenever possible, they worked inside in a special shelter designed for the task.

Yet another summertime chore that fell to women was the tanning of deerskins. The tanning process took at least a day. After the hide had been removed from the animal, it was soaked for some time to soften it, and then it was wrung out. The damp skin was thrown over a post set in the ground at an angle. Using a tool fashioned from bone or stone, the woman then scraped the hide clean of hair and flesh. After cleansing the skin thoroughly once more, she immersed it briefly in a solution made from dried

Ojibwa women and children prepare to harvest berries near their summer camp. Many varieties of wild berries (background) grow in abundance in the Great Lakes region.

deer brain for further softening. In this pliable state, the hide was rinsed and laced to a frame, where it was slowly stretched to its maximum size, then left to dry completely. At this point the deerskin was nearly white. The final step in tanning was smoking the hide to a buttery brown hue, using rotten wood as fuel.

Once tanned, deer hides were fashioned into an assortment of items, including articles of ceremonial value such as tobacco storage bags and drums. Most tanned deerskins were used to make clothing—breech-cloths, leggings, skirts, dresses, and moccasins. To sew such garments, most women used a tough thread of animal sinew. There were special uses for the hides of smaller animals, which were processed with the fur left on. The furry hide of a muskrat was often used to line moccasins, lending warmth and cushioning. Similarly, a rabbit pelt might be placed inside a cradleboard as a soft nestling pad for an infant. Women also wove a kind of blanket from rabbit skin with the fur attached. For this purpose, each skin was cut in a long, continuous strip. Strips cut from many rabbits were then woven together to make a thick, warm covering.

For ceremonial occasions, men might don a tur-banlike headdress made from the pelt of an otter and embellished with ea-gle feathers. Another form of ceremonial headdress was the roach: a crest of animal hair, firmly fastened to an ornately carved bone and adorned with a single feather. Sometimes, men left a lock of their hair long and pulled it through an opening in the bone. Women, for the most part, wore their hair in a simple braid. For ceremonies, they sometimes drew the braid up with a buckskin strip decorated with porcupine quills or beads.

The most basic forms of adornment, however, were tattooing and body painting. Tattooing was performed with sharpened fish or animal bones, dipped in a pigment made from charcoal or clay and inserted under the skin. "This pricking is not done without much pain," one French observer noted. "The spot becomes swollen and sore and even forms a small lump before it heals." Such was the allure of tattooing, however, that some Indians underwent the operation over much of their bodies. Body painting among the tribes of the region was equally elaborate. Men painted themselves for war and for public assemblies, among other solemn occasions.

Standing in a forest clearing, an Ojibwa woman weaves a diamond design into a cedar-bark mat on a simple post frame. Rag rugs were woven using carved wooden heddles, such as this Potawatomi example (right).

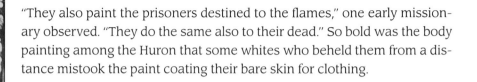

"They also paint the prisoners destined to the flames," one early missionary observed. "They do the same also to their dead." So bold was the body painting among the Huron that some whites who beheld them from a distance mistook the paint coating their bare skin for clothing.

For the Ojibwa and Menominee, in particular, a highlight of the seasonal round was the late-summer harvest of wild rice, which flourished in marshlands from central Wisconsin and Minnesota up into southern Canada and is still gathered by many residents of the region today. Every August, people ventured from their summer camps to the rice fields. By that time, the stalks of the plant were thick and tall, rising up to eight feet out of the water and topped with heavy, barbed spikes. The spikes concealed the kernels of grain. Travelers to the region never failed to be impressed by the sight of the rice, which grew "so thick and luxuriant," in the words of one 19th-century observer, "that the Indians are often obliged to cut passage ways through it for their bark canoes."

Such was the importance of wild rice to the livelihood of the Ojibwa and Menominee that both groups held it sacred and surrounded it with legends and taboos. On winter evenings, elders would relate to the children how the cherished grain had been bequeathed to the tribe. The Ojibwa believed that wild rice had been discovered for them by the fabled trickster Wenebojo, who was known to other tribes of the region by other names. (The Menominee, for example, called him Manabus and said that he had entrusted the plant for safekeeping to members of their Bear Clan.) According to Ojibwa legend, Wenebojo first came upon the grain while on an epic journey to establish his manhood. Although he had been warned against eating anything during his travels, he was tempted by some stalks he saw growing in

An Ojibwa woman carries rolls of birch bark (above) for covering a wig-wam. Women sewed the mats, but men made the bent-sapling frames, such as this one shown partially covered with elm bark (left). Reed matting (below) adds insulation to the roof of a lodge.

AT HOME ANYWHERE

Sauks congregate outside a multifamily summer lodge. The lodge door faces east, which the Sauk call "where daylight appears"; the west is "where the sun goes down," and the wall post to the north is known as "noon."

"We can always say, more truly than thou, that we are at home everywhere because we set up our wigwams with ease wherever we go," explained a 17th-century Algonquian to a Frenchman who suggested that he exchange his bark lodge for a European-style dwelling. Easy to move and extremely durable, the wigwam continued to be the dwelling of choice for migratory groups of Great Lakes Indians for centuries to come.

The basic wigwam, whose name comes from the Algonquian word *wig-wass*, for the birch tree or its bark, consists of a frame of bent saplings covered with sheets of bark and reed matting. But communities created variations on this theme in response to seasonal changes and tribal needs. Most common were the domed winter wigwams *(left)*, whose rounded sides resisted snows and storms. The Ojibwa and others also constructed smaller conical wigwams that were easily transported to temporary camps. In the summer, several tribes moved into airy, gabled houses sided with elm bark *(above)*.

the middle of a lake, which spoke to him and invited him to satisfy his keen hunger. Unable to resist, Wenebojo picked some of the grains and ate them. Miraculously, he did not fall ill. Finally, the stalks spoke to him once more and told Wenebojo their name: *manomin*, or "spirit seed."

The Menominee believed that manomin followed them spontaneously wherever they went. As evidence, they pointed to a lake where wild rice had not grown until the tribe moved to its shores. The Ojibwa said that only the spirits could sow the seed. To assist in that sacred process, they always left some of the rice unharvested, but they long believed that any attempt on the part of humans to cultivate the grain would destroy it. Today some Indians do in fact plant the grains, but they can remember a time when that would have been considered folly. A modern-day Ojibwa explained what his ancestors had taught him: "Man has never planted the rice; it has been put in lakes and rivers, when the land was formed for the Indians. One cannot sow the rice."

A 19th-century Winnebago woman uses a sharp iron tool to soften a deer hide that has been stretched across a wooden frame. After working the white skin, she will sew it into a bag and invert the pouch on a tripod over a smoldering fire of pine, cedar, or corncobs until it is smoked to the desired color.

Strict taboos governed the wild rice harvest. Women could not participate while menstruating. People who had recently lost a family member were prohibited both from gathering the grain and from eating it. Only if they underwent a restorative ceremony might mourners be released from this constraint. To violate these rules would be to alienate the nurturing spirits that made possible the harvest. Moreover, both the Ojibwa and

Menominee believed that underwater monsters lurked in the lakes. If not properly treated, these evil spirits might cause the season's crop to fail. To avoid such a calamity, the Ojibwa staged a ceremony on the evening of the first day's harvest and implored the water spirits not to interfere.

Harvesting the grain became a festive occasion, much like the maple-sugaring season in the spring. Families camped together in small groups along the shores of the rivers and lakes where the rice grew. Each group laid claim to its own spot on the shore and its own stand of rice, to which it returned year after year. People brought little in the way of food with them to the wild rice fields, relying instead on freshly caught fish and waterfowl and the promise of a good harvest.

During the day, the entire family engaged in the hard work of gathering and preparing the rice. But even at the busiest times, there were intervals for relaxation and play, including lacrosse—a pastime the tribes of the western lakes shared with the Iroquois and other woodlands peoples—as well as canoe races, tests of strength, and other diversions. Ojibwa children were especially fond of a spirited contest called the cannibal game, in which a boy was chosen by lot to play the part of the windigo—a dreaded being who lay in wait for his victims like a cunning predator and proceeded to devour them. The boy playing the windigo would cover his head with leaves and hide in the bushes. The other children would then venture forward in a line, guided by their chosen leader, a large boy wielding a club. "When they came near the windigo's hiding place, he rushed out with fearful yells," observed Frances Densmore, an ethnographer who spent many years among the Ojibwas in Minnesota. "The leader fought with him, and the younger children clung screaming to each other. Sometimes the windigo seized a child and pretended to eat it." Such boisterous games relieved the long days of toil at the rice camps. And at night, people young and old indulged in lighthearted storytelling, dancing, and gambling.

The task of bringing in the rice involved several steps, including beating the ripe grains from the stalks with sticks and parching the loosened grains so that the inedible hulls could then be cracked free and winnowed out. Women generally performed most of these chores, while the men ventured out to hunt waterfowl. On occasion, however, men combined the two duties, gliding out in canoes to help gather rice, with their weapons at the ready. Recalled one 20th-century Ojibwa, "My dad, you know, he'd take a gun along and he would go pulling rice and shoot the ducks that'd get up in front of him."

Once the rice harvest was in, the people thanked the spirits for their gift before eating it. Such first-fruit ceremonies are still held to honor the new crop. One Ojibwa recently described the ceremony performed at his community along Minnesota's Nett Lake. Each family head would carry to the house a small container of cooked rice. The containers were tightly covered, since the rice was considered vulnerable to harm from evil spirits until it was blessed. After the pots had been placed on a low table and uncovered, a medicine man lighted a ceremonial pipe and blew tobacco smoke to the four winds as an offering to the spirits (in other versions of this ceremony, grains of rice were blown in the four cardinal directions). Next, an elder offered a prayer, giving thanks that people had been allowed to live another year to enjoy the rice harvest. The medicine man then partook of a small amount of manomin from each pot, followed by the owner. Thus consecrated, the rice was carried home for feasting.

After the harvest, the people of the lakes packed their rice stores in skin pouches or bark containers and returned to their villages. Some of the rice would be carried in containers to the winter camps, and some would be stashed away at the village, like the surplus from the gardens, to nourish the people when they returned the following year. Fishing was a major preoccupation in the fall. Then as winter came on, the men made brief excursions from the village to hunt or trap, while the women made ready for the forthcoming move. Finally, the village broke up once more, and the family groups headed for their scattered hunting camps.

Once snow covered the earth and the waterways froze, families on the move made use of a vehicle the Ojibwa dubbed *nobugidaban,* or "toboggan." These flat-bottomed sleds, which curved up at the front to facilitate movement through the snow, were framed of hardwood that had been felled in the winter when it was free of sap. Tribes in the southern portion of the lakes region subsequently developed heavy toboggans that could be loaded with several people, as well as their gear, and pulled by horses. To the north, however, the forest was too dense and the grazing land too scarce to support horses; when Ojibwas around Lake Superior received a disbursement of saddles from the U.S. government, they served strictly as a source of amusement. Among such northerly groups, as among all tribes of the region in earlier times, toboggans were drawn by hand or by teams of dogs and carried one or two passengers at most, along with a limited load of possessions. The other family members would walk, using snowshoes when the snow lay deep. The snowshoes were framed of hardwood, with a netting composed of hide, twine, or sinew. The Ojibwa called the rounded type of snowshoe the "bear paw" because

A pair of Ojibwa hunters bring ashore their birch-bark canoes with a quarry of deer and waterfowl. A German observer who lived among the Lake Superior Ojibwas commented that these people used canoes "as other nomadic races do horses or camels."

it left a bearlike print in the snow and because legend had it that bears, renowned for their craftiness, once wore such contraptions themselves.

In the winter as in other seasons, Indian hunters of the region relied on various traps and on the bow and arrow. A man heading out in search of quarry sometimes strapped a small toboggan to his back to carry his catch home. He might also bring with him lures to attract animals. (One wooden instrument, used in the spring or summer to attract deer, was fitted with a reed that vibrated when the hunter blew into it, producing a bleating sound reminiscent of a fawn calling its mother.) Certain herbs were also considered effective in attracting game. These hunting charms were usually smoked in a pipe together with a bit of tobacco, producing a penetrating aroma that seemed to lure animals out of hiding. In addition, a hunter might carry a torch to transfix deer and other prey at night.

Ojibwa gamblers threw the four long sticks in a contest of chance known as the snake game. The five shorter pieces were used to keep tally. Also shown are the carrying cases.

Above all, however, the hunter depended on his cunning and persistence. Before stalking prey with bow and arrow, he sometimes fastened an arrowhead lightly to a shaft with sinew. Even if the point did not penetrate too deeply, it was hard to dislodge, for the shaft would snap off as the animal thrashed on the ground or ran through the brush, leaving the flint embedded in the flesh. Then the hunter followed his wounded prey tirelessly, watching for scarlet traces in the snow. Sometimes the pursuit lasted all day, but the hunter seldom lost his quarry once he had drawn blood.

Although hunting might take a man away from his kin for brief periods during the winter, this was the season when the family was closest, confined as they were to their shelters throughout the long, cold nights. When setting up camp, the women covered the pole framework of their wigwams with two layers of mats, one overlapping the other to keep out the wind; panels of birch bark were added to provide extra insulation. The wigwam customarily had just one entrance, and that was covered tightly by a blanket or hide, weighted down with a heavy stick. The only other opening was the smoke hole located above the fireplace. Typically, the father and mother slept on either side of the entrance. To their right and left lay their sons and daughters, respectively, while the opposite side of the shelter from the entrance belonged to the old people. When the weather was especially cold, one of the elders stayed awake until dawn, feeding the fire and watching for sparks.

Before the family members removed their moccasins at night and settled down to sleep with their feet toward the fire, children played

Winnebago women of Black River Falls, Wisconsin, play a traditional game with bone dice; before them are small beans used to keep score. The player on the left has placed a white cloth over her head, probably because she did not wish to be photographed.

games and adults busied themselves with handiwork. The men might repair their snowshoes, while the women knotted twine into fishnets. Above all, the evening was a time for weaving stories, an art at which the old women excelled. Sometimes the storytellers dramatized their accounts by circling the fire, grimacing and gesturing to the beat of a drum. They told of a world filled with manitous—spirit powers that took innumerable forms. In no season were the people closer to those mysterious forces than in midwinter. To the Ojibwa, January was known as Gitci-manitou-gizis, or the Big Spirit Moon. In that haunting time, when the wolves howled at night and the chill wind moaned, the families in their shelters knew that all the ingenuity bequeathed to them by their ancestors was not enough in itself to sustain them. It was only through the mercy of higher powers that they found warmth and safety in the bitter depths of the year. ◆

GRAIN FROM THE SPIRIT OF THE LAKE

Every year, at the blessing of the first fruits of the wild rice harvest, an elder would recite this prayer: "Thank you spirit that again we come to see this rice that you must have offered to the Indian for him to eat." Underlying that age-old invocation was the belief that manomin, wild rice, belonged uniquely to the Indians, a food that nourished their culture as well as their bodies.

Among the Ojibwa and the Menominee, in whose tribal marshlands most of the rice grew, the traditional late-summer harvest served as a reminder of the obligations they owed to the spirits, to the earth, and to each other. They marked out family plots in the rice field, guaranteeing everyone a share in the harvest. As they worked, they let grains fall into the water as an offering to the spirit of the lake. And they were careful not to damage the plants and so diminish next year's crop.

In the early years of the 20th century, when the following photographs were taken on reservations in Minnesota and Wisconsin, the old ways still prevailed. Even today, many Ojibwas and Menominees look forward to "making rice," taking vacations from their jobs and returning to their ancestral lands in order to harvest and prepare rice for their families, and for sale to others, in the traditional way.

"As our boat glides on the water, we pause to see where the rice looks the darkest to determine where it is the ripest," observes Norma Smith, an Ojibwa from Wisconsin. "Then one partner readies for the first swipe at the tall stalks. How good to hear the first rice hit the apron."

A woman's forked pole allows her to navigate the wild rice fields without damaging the roots of the plants. The 19th-century engraving by Seth Eastman (inset) is somewhat fanciful—three people in a canoe would leave insufficient room for the rice.

BINDING THE STALKS

A few weeks before the harvest, women went out to bind the stalks of wild rice in their family plots. In these photos, Mary Razer of White Earth Reservation, Minnesota, prepares her binding string from strips of basswood bark (above) and then ties rice stalks together (right). Ownership of the sheaves was shown by the color or pattern of the binding.

Binding a sheaf of wild rice (above) protects the grains from birds and makes collecting the rice easier—harvesters simply untie the sheaves and shake or brush the ripe kernels directly into the boat. At left is a bundle of basswood-bark twine that was used to bind the sheaves.

REAPING THE HARVEST

In customary fashion, a man poles the boat while a woman uses a pair of lightweight ricing sticks, like the ones shown at left, to harvest the grain. With one stick she bends the stalks gently over the gunwales; with the other she brushes or knocks the ripe kernels into the bottom of the boat.

At Lac Court Oreilles, Wisconsin, Alice White Cadotte aims a light, glancing stroke with her ricing stick that will remove the ripe kernels without breaking the stalks. Each blow of the ricing stick harvests about a quarter of a pint of kernels; five minutes' work usually yields a pound of rice. After two hours, a boat like the one pictured below might be filled with wild rice more than a foot deep.

PROCESSING THE KERNELS

Freshly harvested rice mildews quickly if not dried. Above, a Minnesota Ojibwa woman dries the rice kernels following the usual method—exposing the grains to light and air on a birch-bark mat and constantly turning them with a wooden paddle like the one pictured above right. Drying the rice on a scaffold (right) over a slow-burning fire also cures the grain so it does not need to be parched later.

In birch-bark baskets such as the one at left, the Indians carried the dried rice to the parching kettles. Parching, or roasting, the grain (above) prevents the kernel from sprouting, loosens the hull so it can be discarded easily, and preserves the rice.

Grasping two poles for support, an Ojibwa youth treads rice in a "bootaagan," a 2- to 3-foot-deep pit lined with wooden slats. Raising his knees high and twisting his feet in what resembles a dance, he presses the rice against the abrasive surface of the slats to break the hull and free the kernel from the chaff. Below, in an alternative method, three women use wooden pestles to pound the rice in a bark container.

A mortar and pestle (above) might also be used to hull wild rice. The pestle was probably made of a soft wood such as poplar.

WINNOWING THE CHAFF

Holding light, shallow birch-bark winnowing trays called "nooshkaachinaaganan" (shown at right), two women toss batches of hulled rice into the air to let the wind disperse the paper-thin chaff. A dry, sunny, breezy day is ideal for winnowing.

STORING RICE FOR THE WINTER

Prudent Indian families kept a plentiful store of wild rice in huts like this one. Wild rice was a year-round staple, a life-saver during hard winters, and a commodity for trade.

The Ojibwa and Menominee stored wild rice in bags and baskets made from the inner bark of cedar or birch trees. The rice was covered with a layer of hay and the mouth of the bag sewn shut with basswood fiber. Kept dry, wild rice will last indefinitely.

BUILDING A BARK CANOE

The French explorer Samuel de Champlain was the son of a sea captain and a lifelong ocean voyager, but he was astonished by the watercraft he first saw on the Saint Lawrence River in 1603. Two bark-covered canoes, each paddled by two Indians, easily outsped and outmaneuvered his fully manned longboat, however his oarsmen strained. Champlain became the first European to advocate that his countrymen adopt this light and maneuverable vessel for their own purposes.

It is not known how or when bark canoes were first developed; no ancient examples or records exist. They sprang into recorded history fully evolved, so elegantly refined to their purpose that in four succeeding centuries, no significant improvement has been made on their design, one that affords light weight (important on portages), shallow draft for shallow waters, carrying capacity, strength, and durability.

Manufactured with simple implements from plant materials, the bark canoe was neither fragile nor crude. Because its wooden ribs and planks were split, they were stronger and more flexible than sawed wood. The com-

bination of elasticity and light weight found in the bark of the paper birch, the canoe covering widely used by the Great Lakes Indians, has not been surpassed by modern materials. The joinery, painstakingly fitted and bound with split tree roots, was as tough as any done with modern tools and fasteners. And the final product was a triumph of grace and beauty.

Although Indian bark canoes typically measured about 20 feet in length, there were many variations—some based on tribal custom, most based on function. Hunters probing small streams overhung by dense foliage used eight-foot, low-ended models. Those braving white water or large lakes needed soaring bows and sterns to ward off turbulent water and favored deep, V-shaped hulls to hold a course. Warriors wanted narrow hulls for speed; freighters preferred a wide beam for carrying capacity (when the

fur trade was at its height, some canoes were made as long as 36 feet and capable of transporting four tons).

Canoe routes stretched all the way from the Atlantic Ocean to the Pacific, requiring portages of at most a dozen miles or so. But no region was more accessible to paddlers than the Great Lakes area, with its ubiquitous watercourses. There, canoe building was a craft of supreme importance and refinement.

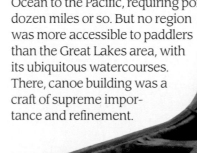

The highly crafted utilitarian beauty of the bark canoe, such as this Ojibwa model, suggested to 19th-century naturalist Henry David Thoreau a "long antiquity in which its manufacture has been gradually perfected."

A modern canoe builder strips bark from a birch in northern Minnesota (left). The stripped tree will survive, its white replaced with dark-colored scar tissue. The bindings of each canoe consisted of pencil-thick black spruce roots—grubbed from swampy ground (above), then trimmed, debarked, and split.

GATHERING THE RAW MATERIALS

The trees whose wood and bark were best for a canoe—birch, cedar, and spruce—abounded in the moist ground near the waterways of the northern forest. Especially in the centuries before white people appeared, the supply seemed inexhaustible. But it was not easy to collect the building materials.

After finding a large expanse of unblemished bark on a straight tree, canoe builders had to assess its flexibility and thickness. According to one modern artisan, finding the 20 or so pieces of bark needed for a single canoe involves surveying a square mile of birch trees.

The cedar used for a canoe's ribs, planks, thwarts, and gunwales had to be free of knots and twists so the craftsmen could readily split the pieces to thicknesses as little as one-eighth of an inch. In all, as much as two-thirds of the total building time was devoted to finding and preparing the materials.

Indian canoe builders roll out a fresh piece of birch bark and flatten it with rocks in order to prevent curling; this procedure was used when the canoe was not to be built immediately. To avoid puncturing the bark, only flat, smooth stones were used.

A modern Ojibwa canoe builder using a steel knife in place of the traditional stone wedge splits a batten of northern white cedar to form a canoe's ribs (above). Cedar was prized for this purpose because, when thoroughly seasoned, it splits cleanly and easily. An average canoe required 40 or 50 ribs, which had to be soaked in boiling water so they could be bent to shape (right).

PREPARING THE CRAFT'S SKELETON

On a shaded bed of firm earth, cleared of rocks and roots, Indian canoe builders began by shaping and lashing together the gunwales—the top edge of the canoe—with carved crosspieces, or thwarts, mortised in place. The result was the gunwale frame, which dictated the length and width of the finished canoe, as well as the curvature of its edge.

Until the advent of Europeans, Indi-ans felled the trees they needed with fire; split the pieces to size with wedges and knives of flint, jasper, or bone, sometimes driven with wooden mauls; shaped thwarts and paddles by abrading the wood with chisels and scrapers fashioned from bone, shell, or beaver's teeth; and drilled holes with awls made from deer antlers. The appearance of steel knives did not improve—but merely accelerated—the workmanship.

Workers drive stakes into the earth around the outline of the gunwale frame. The next step was to remove the stakes and set them aside with the frame in order to place the birch bark on the building bed.

Rachel Daugherty, wife and daughter of Potawatomi canoe builders in Michigan (left), surveys a canoe taking shape on the building bed. The gunwale frame has been raised into place (below) and has been bent upward at each end to establish the sheer, or upper profile, of the canoe. The birch bark has been shaped to the frame and fixed in place temporarily with stakes.

Having spread the birch bark on the building bed and replaced the gunwale frame within the outline of the stake holes, artisans place heavy rocks on the frame to hold it in place while the bark is shaped around it.

SHAPING THE SKIN

Contrary to popular illustration, a birch-bark canoe was made with the white outer surface of the bark on the inside of the vessel and the tan inner surface facing outward. Unlike modern boatbuilders, Indian craftsmen formed the outer covering before placing the inner planks and ribs.

As the bark was bent upward to the shape of the frame, the builder sometimes cut slits in the material and overlapped it to avoid wrinkles. Often, additional pieces of bark had to be stitched on to cover the beam's widest section.

With a canoe-shaped bark envelope formed, the craftsmen raised the gunwale frame approximately a foot, establishing the vessel's freeboard, and set it on wood posts. They then fastened the bark to the frame by adding an outer rim of wood to the gunwale and pegging it down. Once they had fitted the bow and stern with bark deck flaps, they could begin the lashing.

Craftsmen fold the bark up to the gunwale frame, holding it in place by tying opposite stakes together on the inside, and shaping the frame with splints placed crosswise on the stakes against the outside of the hull.

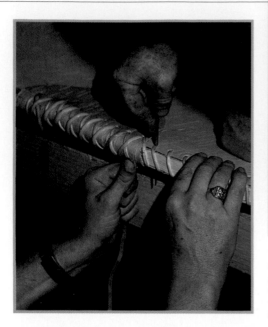

While a helper holds the pieces taut (left), a modern builder cross-stitches bark to the prow of a nearly completed canoe. After stitching is complete and the inner planks have been set in place (above), the ribs are pressed into place, their ends slipping into the open sections of the inner gunwale.

Ojibwa women use split spruce roots to lash together the inner and outer pieces of the gunwale, at the same time stitching the bark into place between the pieces. They leave spaces between the sections of binding for insertion of the ribs. Bent stem pieces have been inserted that will give the distinctive, graceful curved shape to both bow and stern.

STITCHING AND SPLICING

It took 500 feet of split black spruce root to complete the bindings of a typical birch-bark canoe. The pencil-size roots were debarked, split lengthwise, and then stored in water to keep them flexible until they were needed. The roots were applied with their flat side against the surfaces of the boat, the rounded side outward.

Bindings were passed through holes punched in the bark with awls to secure the covering to the gunwales and stem pieces. Each end of the length of root used was tucked under adjacent wrappings to hold it fast. To splice pieces of bark together, women usually used a cross-stitch, sometimes reinforcing the seam with a thin wood batten. Splices were made with the overlap facing the stern, so that the seam would not be torn open when the canoe scraped over a rock. Thus the canoes, although symmetrical, were not reversible.

Workers insert cedar planks along the length of the canoe to form a hull inside the bark covering. Two dozen or more planks, each split to a thickness of about one-eighth of an inch, were placed so that they over-lapped in the midsection by six inches. Some Indian groups lapped each plank over its neighbor, while others laid the planks flush.

A modern canoe builder smears pitch on a seam. Many of today's craftsmen, in a departure from tradition, use asphalt pitch instead of spruce gum, because the latter is difficult to prepare and not as effective.

While a woman tends a pot of heated spruce pitch, two others use the substance to seal stitched seams in a canoe's bark skin. If a seam cracked, a traveler could make repairs by chewing a wad of spruce resin until it was pliable, then applying it with a hot stick.

SEALING THE SEAMS

The final step in making a canoe seaworthy—sealing the stitched seams in the bark—was the only one for which early Indian builders did not have an entirely satisfactory material. The Indians scraped resin from fallen or damaged spruce trees, or collected it in a wound made in a standing tree's bark, then heated it and skimmed off impurities. The resulting pitch cracked in cold weather and melted in hot, so it had to be tempered with judicious amounts of animal fat and charcoal.

A last round of touch-ups to the canoe included stuffing the bow and stern with shavings or moss held in with headboards (to help keep the vessel buoyant when loaded down) and pegging strips of wood on top of the gunwales to protect the lashings. Before launching, the bow might be decorated with a personal or tribal symbol. Then, perhaps a fortnight after the work began, the canoe was ready for the water.

An Ojibwa woman, photographed in the 1980s (above), enjoys the maiden voyage of a just-completed canoe.

2

THE REALM OF THE MANITOUS

Puppets such as these Menominee figures, attached to sticks, were manipulated by shamans of the Great Lakes region in ceremonies intended to help heal illness, bring lovers together, and produce other beneficial effects.

"The story that I'm going to tell you won't be about this earth. It will be about a different world." So begins an Ojibwa account of the birth of Wenebojo, the fabled trickster and wonder-worker who was celebrated by many tribes of the region under one name or another. Before Wenebojo was born, the story goes, there were just two lonely beings "living in this other world: an old lady and her daughter." For food, they had only the berries the girl gathered in the fields. Morning after morning, she went out on her own to harvest the ripe fruit. Then one day, as she labored beneath the noontime sun, a gust of wind sprang up and lifted the skirt that covered her. She thought nothing of it at the time, the tale relates, "because no one was there to see her." When she returned home with her pickings, however, her mother sensed a change in her.

"When you go out every day to gather berries," the old woman asked, "do you ever see anybody out there?"

"No," her daughter answered. "I'm all by myself all day."

But soon the girl herself began to sense a change. Something had happened to her, but all she could remember was the glare of the noontime sun and the gust of wind. She told her mother about it, and the old lady knew at once what had taken place: The spirit of the sun had gazed down on the girl from above and possessed her with the help of the wind.

Shortly thereafter, the girl left her mother and went off into the woods, where she gave birth to three baby boys—one who looked quite human, a second who looked less human, and a third who had nothing human about him and was made of stone. The firstborn was Wenebojo, and he grew up strong and fierce. According to the legend, "he killed everything he could kill, even the little birds." When he had hunted all around, he

yearned to travel to distant lands, but he was held back by his youngest brother, the boy of stone, who could not move.

"I will kill our brother," Wenebojo told the second-born, "and then we won't have to stay in this one place anymore." Wenebojo attacked the boy of stone with a poleax, but he only wore out his weapon. At length, the victim spoke up and told Wenebojo how to destroy him: "Build a fire, put me in, and when I get to look like a red-hot coal, throw some water on me." Wenebojo did as he was told and cracked his youngest brother into pieces.

Then Wenebojo and his surviving sibling were free to roam. "They had no special place to come back to now," the tale relates. "They traveled all the time." Eventually, the younger brother tired of wandering and began to lag behind. Once again, Wenebojo yearned to be free of restraint.

"Brother, can't you wait for me here a few days?" he asked impatiently. "After four days I'll come back." To keep his brother safe until he returned, Wenebojo dug a hole for him and covered him up, leaving a stone there to mark the place. But Wenebojo did not come back in four days: "He traveled and traveled and traveled. He went just as fast as he could, because there was no one to hold him back now." When he finally remembered his brother and returned for him, it was too late: Spirits had claimed

Dressed in clothing that reflects enduring native traditions, an Ojibwa family gathers in its wigwam in 1935. Among the tribal lore passed down from generation to generation within the home were haunting stories of the spirit world.

him, and he was on his way to the next world, a journey that took him across a river spanned by a slippery log that was really a snake. Henceforth, all humans would have to follow that path when they died. Wenebojo regretted the loss of his brother, but once he had paid his respects, he was too hungry for adventure to be weighed down by thoughts of those he had dispensed with. "Now that Wenebojo was all alone," the tale attests, "he traveled wherever he wanted to go."

This recent version of the old Wenebojo legend, related to folklorist Victor Barnouw by an Ojibwa holy man and storyteller who went by the name of Tom Badger, tells of a trait that long helped the people of the lakes survive under trying circumstances—a readiness to leave behind familiar surroundings and seek out fresh opportunities. Much as Indians of the region prized such venturesomeness, however, they also knew that misfortune awaited those who pursued their own ends and ignored the ties that bound them to the kindred spirits all around. They realized that Wenebojo was not truly on his own after the death of his brothers, any more than his mother was alone when she went out to pick berries. For the world was alive with the mysterious beings called manitous. No one could elude the majestic powers aloft, such as the sun and the four winds, or the bountiful spirits that inhabited the earth and watched over the animals and the growing things, or the often-deadly forces that lurked in the watery depths.

Wenebojo himself was descended from spirits, but he resembled humans in his reckless pride. Ever eager to prove himself against rival powers, he sometimes met with humiliating setbacks. Yet his mishaps were no less instructive to the people than his triumphs. By following his ups and downs, youngsters learned to temper boldness with caution. Through Wenebojo, they learned their place in society and in the world.

Even some of Wenebojo's most foolish acts brought unforeseen benefits to the people. As Tom Badger related, Wenebojo once succeeded in snaring some fowl by building a lodge and inviting them to a dance. As the birds entered the lodge, the trickster shook his rattle and proclaimed: "I want you all to close your eyes. Anybody that opens his eyes will have funny-looking red eyes forever." His guests complied, and as they sang and danced, Wenebojo proceeded to wring their necks, one by one. Finally, a loon who had joined in the festivities grew wary and opened his eyes. He cried out a warning, and the surviving birds flew from Wenebojo's grasp. The loon escaped too, but he and his descendants paid a price—they had funny-looking red eyes thereafter. As for Wenebojo, his glee was hardly diminished by the loss of a few birds. He was so pleased with himself, in fact, that he grew careless. That night, he put the dead birds on a fire to roast and curled up by the flames to sleep, leaving it to his rear end to watch for intruders. Sure enough, thieves crept up in the dark and made off with his catch. (The Ojibwa said that these stealthy beings came from the south wind, while the Menominee likened them to the Winnebago, their furtive rivals to the south.)

When he awoke and found his dinner gone, Wenebojo was beside himself with rage. He blamed his rear end for failing to sound the alarm. As Tom Badger put it, he was determined "to give his hind end a lesson," so he thrust it into the fire. Soon, his bones were crackling, and Wenebojo began to feel that the punishment was too much. So he walked off into the bush, where his burning flesh set some weeds afire. Wenebojo looked behind him and saw fragrant smoke rising to the heavens. He had discovered tobacco—a gift for which humankind would remain eternally grateful. Afterward, some of Wenebojo's charred flesh fell to the ground, where it formed a lichen that women later gathered in times of want and made into a porridge. Thus people profited greatly from Wenebojo's misadventure.

Wenebojo endowed humans with other assets as well. He was the first who dared to eat wild rice, and he showed people how to make use of many other precious plants and tools. His great legacy, however, was to teach humans how to deal with the animals that lived all around them. As a hunter, Wenebojo relied more on subterfuge than on brute strength. Once when he spied a moose in the distance, he threw the animal off its guard by claiming to be its long-lost kinsman. "Brother, so this is where you are!" he called out to the moose. "I've been looking all over for you! We were brought up by different people when we were small babies, so it's a long time since I last saw you. You

This weathered Ojibwa effigy of the mid-1800s may represent a protective spirit, or manitou. Such carvings were displayed outside the home to keep the family safe; passersby sometimes placed clothing or ornaments on the figure in order to honor the manitou.

Ojibwas draped clothing over the branches of "offering" trees like this one to ward off misfortune. The clothing was offered to the sky manitous to secure their blessings.

wouldn't remember me." Intrigued, the lone moose drew closer, and Wenebojo asked him if he had heard the news about the fellow who killed his brother. The moose was curious and wanted to know how it happened. So Wenebojo had the animal stand sideways with his head averted. Then he drew his bow and shot the moose in the flank. "What are you doing, Wenebojo?" his victim cried out. "You're killing me." To which the trickster replied: "Well, brother, I told you as much."

The Great Lakes tribes admired such cunning, for they knew that hunters lived by their wits. Some people even imitated Wenebojo when tracking their prey. In one incident observed by an ethnographer in the late 19th century, an Ojibwa boarded a canoe with his wife and paddled after a moose that had jumped into a lake to escape pursuing wolves. As the man closed in on the moose, he made ready to slit its throat. But all the while, he was calling out to it in a soothing voice, "Don't worry, we want to get acquainted with you."

Despite such stratagems, the Indians of the lakes region never forgot that all members of each species were watched over by a guardian manitou that was sympathetic to respectful humans. For that reason, people felt beholden to the animals they stalked and honored them in their prayers and in their stories. Although Wenebojo appeared to be callous in the extreme when he called the moose he was about to slay his "brother," many tales told about the fabled trickster confirm that he was closely related to the creatures around him. Indeed, he could take the form of any animal at will, be it a grasping predator or an elusive prey. He sometimes appeared as a hare—an animal the Indians never ceased to marvel at as it dashed through the snow in winter, all but invisible to its foes. In that guise, the trickster was known to some Indians as the Great Hare.

Wenebojo's profound kinship with animals was the theme of one of the most compelling legends told about him. Sometime after he fooled the moose, it was said, Wenebojo came upon a pack of timber wolves—one old one and several younger ones—and tried to deceive them in the same manner. "Brothers, come here," he called out. "I've walked all over, looking for you. I heard that you were around here somewhere. The last time I saw you we were babies. You wouldn't remember me." But when the wolves came closer, Wenebojo discovered that he had met his match. These restless hunters were indeed his kin. "The wolves had no place that they could call home," related Tom Badger. "They traveled just like Wenebojo did." So the trickster joined the pack. The old wolf became his guardian and the young ones became his siblings.

When the pack ventured out on long journeys, however, Wenebojo found to his dismay that he could barely keep up. The old wolf reluctantly concluded that they must leave Wenebojo behind, but he kindly offered him the company of his favorite wolf brother so that Wenebojo could rest while his kinsman prowled for food. One evening, the young wolf failed to return from his hunting. Wenebojo went out after him, following in his tracks until they ended ominously by a river. The wolf had fallen prey to treacherous water spirits.

For the first time, Wenebojo was overcome by grief. He raged against the destructive manitous and swore to avenge his wolf brother. He carved a great bow from a cedar log and cut two arrows, one for each of the spirits that ruled in the depths. Then he sought out a sandy bank where those manitous were said to emerge in the form of snakes to bask in the sun on fine days. There Wenebojo lay in wait, disguised as a tree stump.

In time, the two deadly manitous appeared. "I've never seen that stump before," one great snake said to the other as they slithered ashore. "Maybe that's Wenebojo. He does everything."

"That can't be Wenebojo," the other spirit replied. "He isn't enough of a manitou to do that."

But his companion remained suspicious. So he coiled himself around the stump and squeezed as hard as he could. The pressure was so great that Wenebojo nearly gave himself away before the snake relented. "That's not Wenebojo," the manitou declared. Reassured, he and his companion fell asleep in the sun. Whereupon Wenebojo resumed his human form, drew his great bow, and mortally wounded his two enemies.

The demise of the manitous so disturbed the waters they ruled over

Indians confront two serpents and a water monster called Michipeshu—capable of whipping up storms—in a rock painting on the Ontario shore of Lake Superior. The people of the lakes tried to placate such water spirits through prayers and gifts of tobacco.

that a great flood arose. Wenebojo climbed the highest mountain, then the highest tree on the mountain, and just managed to keep his head above water. From his perch, he looked around and saw that a few other resourceful creatures had survived the deluge—the otter, the beaver, and the muskrat. "Brothers," he called out, "could you go down and get some earth? If you do, I will make a world for you and me to live on." The otter and the beaver tried and failed, but the muskrat succeeded in bringing up a bit of earth, and from that clump Wenebojo made a floating island that grew ever bigger and became the world we know today.

Some say that Wenebojo grew even more daring after this great feat and defied all the enduring spirits, above and below. He was still grieving for his brother the wolf, and he had no fear of any competing power. "Whoever is underneath the earth down there," he declared, "I will pull them out and bring them up on top here. I can play with them and do whatever I want with them, because I own this earth." Likewise, he defied the spirits above. "Whoever is up there," he shouted to the sky, "I will get them and pull them down. I will play with them here and do just as I please with them. I will even knock down the sky."

Alarmed by Wenebojo's threats, the greatest of the manitous below the earth met with the greatest of the spirits above the earth, and the two came up with a plan. They decided that Wenebojo needed kin to watch over him. He had done away with his own brothers and lost his kinsman the wolf. For all his accomplishments, he remained young and impetuous. So the spirits sent to him a mother and father—the first people on earth. They were not his true parents: He called the woman his aunt and the man his uncle. Yet they helped him find his place in the world. And all the people who descended from that first couple knew they too would have to learn their rightful place—between the spirits above and the spirits below, and between the older generation and the younger one. When they did so, they would share in the wisdom that came even to reckless Wenebojo in time. As Tom Badger remarked: "Wenebojo is still alive and can hear what we're saying right now. He's probably laughing when he thinks about how he lived when he was young and about all the foolish things he did."

As illustrated by the adventures of Wenebojo, the people of the lakes inhabited a world that was home to an array of spirits who might be either helpful or harmful, depending on their disposition and on how they were treated. Fortunately, infants entering this complex universe did not have to make their own way like Wenebojo and deal with the manitous alone.

An Ojibwa mother holds her infant in a cradleboard, equipped with a wooden hoop to protect the child's head. Parents dangled objects of spiritual significance from the hoop for the infant to admire—including gifts from the elder who named the child.

From the start, they were guided by their elders. And as they proceeded on their spiritual journey—a pilgrimage that lasted a lifetime and continued even after death—they were strengthened by the rituals of family, clan, and community, all of which served to keep individuals on the true path.

Traditionally, the first direct involvement of the child in the ritual life of the tribe came in the form of the naming ceremony. Among the Ojibwa, the parents asked an older man or woman of good reputation to bestow on their child a name—and, by extension, the blessings of the manitous that the elder had enjoyed. At a feast held when the child was one month old, the elder recounted for the assembled family and friends the benefits he or she had received from the spirits. In particular, the elder spoke of a special power received during a vision quest, which was customarily conducted about the time of puberty. It was this power and this identity that the elder was conveying temporarily to the child until the youngster matured. After announcing the name, the elder embraced the infant and joined the company in a feast and in prayers for the child's long life and good health.

The name thus conveyed was important in the ritual life of the child thereafter. An Ojibwa namer bestowed on the child a token gift that would remain among the individual's sacred possessions. Youngsters were watched closely for any aberrant behavior that might indicate they had been given a ceremonial name that did not suit them. The ceremonial name was seldom if ever used in daily life. Instead, the child was referred to by a nickname that alluded to some characteristic trait or behavior. A girl who scratched her playmates when they pestered her might become known as Little Cat, for example, while a boy who kept to himself might receive the nickname Stands Alone.

An infant spent the major part of the first year of life bound to a cradleboard. With feet placed against a footboard and head protected by a loop of hickory, the snugly wrapped baby could be carried on its mother's back or propped against a tree as she worked. Mothers cut holes in the soles of the infant's moccasins so that any spirit tempted to claim the new life would relent when it found that the moccasins were in no condition for the journey to the afterworld.

Infants were seldom weaned before the age of three or four, and toddlers were treated indulgently by their family. There were taboos against striking children, or even subjecting them to harsh criticism. As befitted a society where leaders influenced people by setting an example rather than by issuing orders, parents were models of firmness and fairness for children to emulate. When youngsters persisted in misbehaving, parents encouraged obedience by telling them stories of animals and manitous that would harm wayward children. Youngsters playing in dangerous areas were frightened off with a scarecrow or a family member wearing a hideous mask, and children who refused to settle down at night were told that an owl would carry them off and eat them if they did not go to sleep.

Until the age of 10 or so, a child's life was spent learning and practicing the skills of adulthood under the supervision of the extended family. Each child had many guardians; the term *mother* was applied to the birth mother and her sisters, and the term *father* to the natural father and his brothers. Through stories, games, and playacting, fathers and uncles taught boys the rudiments of hunting, while mothers and aunts introduced girls to their responsibilities. Girls learned to make and care for cornhusk dolls, for example, while boys practiced with toy bows and arrows. In time, boys were allowed to accompany their elders on real hunts. When a youngster killed his first animal, the entire family joined in a celebratory feast dedicated to the spirit guardian of that species.

In training their youngsters, parents made little distinction between spiritual and practical lessons, for all useful skills were said to come from the manitous. Before they were old enough to help gather materials for the building of a canoe, for example, boys and girls learned to be thankful for

Red wool covers this horse effigy, carved by a Potawatomi of Wisconsin in the 19th century. By then, horses were a common sight in the lakes region and were celebrated in legends and lore.

the spirits that gave of themselves to make the task possible. According to one Ojibwa tale that was passed down from generation to genera-tion, Wenebojo built the first canoe after meeting in council with the trees of the forest and appealing to them for assistance. The birch agreed to do-nate its sturdy bark for the skin of the craft, the cedar kindly volunteered timber for the frame, the tamarack contributed its roots to tie up the bark, and the pine consented to "shed a few tears of pitch to cement the whole together and make it waterproof."

Such inspirational tales were told during the long winter evenings, when the youngsters gathered around the fire in the snug wigwam and listened to elders who had spent a lifetime memorizing the lore of the tribe. "I have known some Indians," recalled one Ojibwa, "who could com-mence to relate legends and stories in the month of October and not end until quite late in the spring, and on every evening of this long term tell a new story." Tales of a sacred nature were never recounted during the warmer months, when dangerous underwater spirits emerged in the guise of snakes and frogs. A wise person did not speak of sacred things again until such creatures went back into hiding late in the year.

Learning the identities and propensities of the manitous was as im-portant to youngsters as getting to know their human neighbors and kin. The most remote of the manitous were those that resided high up in the sky—the spirits of the male sun and the female moon and the four winds. The sun and the moon were thought of as great and good, while the four winds brought changes in the weather and in the seasons that might be either beneficial or calamitous. In the air below the domain of the highest manitous hovered the spirits of the birds, from the sacred eagle to the fear-some owl and the awe-inspiring thunderbird. That fabled being, which struck thunder from its wings and hurled lightning bolts from its talons, was not always to be dreaded. It could confer power on warriors and

chiefs, for example. On earth dwelt the spirits that supervised the animals and either helped or hindered hunters, along with the manitous that controlled harvests, presided over specific rituals or cures, or inhabited certain mysterious features such as strangely shaped rocks. At the lowest level—beneath the surface of lakes and rivers and beneath the floating island of the earth itself—lurked the fearsome manitous that caused drownings, floods, and other misfortunes.

Other terrible beings were said to lurk in the forest or at the ends of the earth. Chief among them was the windigo, a monster who devoured humans or took control of them. People possessed by the windigo became cannibals themselves. One sign that an individual had been touched by the windigo was gluttony, and children were cautioned to eat moderately or risk being regarded as likely cannibals. Some people who were falling under the windigo's influence tried to protect those around them from the consequences. In the early 20th century, the Ojibwas who lived on Parry Island in Georgian Bay told of a strange old man who was sometimes seen sharpening sticks on which to roast people. Fortunately, the old man knew in advance when the evil hunger was coming on and warned others away. As one neighbor remarked gratefully, "He died before he became a real

An Ojibwa couple sit side by side at the time of their marriage in 1869, with well-wishers in the background. "You will share the same fire," an Ojibwa husband and wife were told when they married. "You will walk the same trail."

windigo." Sometimes described as being made of ice, the windigo was most to be feared in winter, when any prolonged period of bad luck on the part of the hunters left people prey to starvation and dreadful cravings.

Knowledge of the spirit world came to youngsters not only from stories but also from dreams. Children were encouraged to remember their dreams and speak of them, for dreams often brought messages from the manitous. "In the old days," one Ojibwa remarked, "our people had no education. They could not learn from books nor from teachers. All their wisdom and knowledge came to them in dreams. They tested their dreams, and in that way learned their own strength."

By the time they reached puberty, youngsters were ready to seek out the special dream, or vision, that would define them as adults. Among the Great Lakes peoples as among tribes elsewhere in North America, this vision quest was the height of religious experience and was often preceded by fasting. Children were tested with an offering of food, often accompanied by one of charcoal; youngsters who were ready for the quest rejected the food and marked their faces with charcoal to signify a fast. Such self-denial, which children practiced for short periods even before puberty, prepared them not only for the vision quest but also for the ritual fasting that warriors underwent before battle and for the privation that hunters and their kin had to endure patiently in lean times.

As the time for the quest approached, parents and elders frequently offered specific instruction about the kind of vision to be expected and what it might mean. They offered examples of good and powerful visions, contrasted with dangerous or useless results. Proper timing was essential. A vision pursued by a child not yet mature enough to understand it could cause illness, while delaying the quest for too long could leave a child lethargic for life. Quests were seldom carried out in summer, because a call to the spirit world then might be answered by the underwater manitous. The transitional times of late fall or early spring were regarded as the proper seasons for the quest.

Youngsters of both sexes sought visions in this way. For girls, the experience sometimes coincided with the period of fasting and isolation at the time of their first menstruation. Alternatively, girls might venture out as boys did in search of a vision. In such cases, a parent often escorted the child to a secluded hilltop—the Menominee had a small lodge built for the purpose—or a platform built in a tree, where solitude would be absolute and uninterrupted. There the youngster waited and fasted, except for a little nourishment taken after five days. Success was expected after about 10 days, but was by no means assured. Sometimes it was necessary to try again and again, and in rare cases, no vision ever appeared and the youngster was regarded as uninspired. Occasionally, a vision was rejected as inappropriate, and another try was made.

Although much depended on this vision quest, children were urged not to ask the spirits for too much. A legend handed down by the Winnebago told of a youngster who sought a vision of the creator, Maona. This was unwise, for Maona, or Earth Maker, could be seen only through his creations. Nonetheless, the youth "blackened his face, as was the custom, and fasted four days or more, and dreamed of many things; then he ate a little food and fasted again. So he persevered until he had dreamed of everything on the earth and under the earth, or in the air; he dreamed of the whole world, but he never saw Maona." At length, a voice told him to be satisfied and end his quest: "You have dreamed of Maona because you have dreamed of all his works."

Yet the stubborn young man persisted, until at last a spirit claiming to be Maona appeared before him and promised him immortality: "You can never die, because you are like me. You have dreamed of all my works, you know them all, and so you are like me." As the spirit departed, however, the youngster could see "that it was only a chicken hawk, one of the evil spirit's birds." The youngster cried in sorrow and continued his fast until the voice spoke to him again in warning: "Cease trying to dream of Maona. There are many more little birds and creatures of the evil spirit that may deceive you. You can dream no more, for you have seen all things."

In this instance, the youngster who sought too great a dream suffered only discouragement. But one Ojibwa legend told of a boy who, having already experienced a vision, continued to fast at the urging of his father in order to increase his power. The manitous turned him into a robin. Others who searched too long and hard for a vision risked becoming murderers or madmen. In the quest for inspiration, as in all things, the people of the lakes counseled moderation.

In most cases, seekers who fasted devoutly aroused the pity of the spirits and were granted a vision that inspired them ever after. This vision was seldom spoken of. One might discuss it with one's father or with a shaman—young Menominees were expected to go to the shaman for a full interpretation—but to tell of the vision was to summon the manitous, something not to be done casually. As a result, visions were rarely set down in writing. The few that have been recorded, however, have a common outcome: the appearance of a being who might take any form—ani-

Ojibwas perform a scalp dance after a mock
battle at Minnesota's White Earth Reservation in 1910. During such ceremonies, men
proclaimed their spirit power by singing
songs and raising poles topped with enemy
scalps like the one at left, claimed from a
Dakota Sioux in the 19th century and
adorned with feathers and a beaded band.

mal, human, or supernatural—and who offered the seeker compassion, insight, good fortune, and lifelong spiritual guidance.

In one vision, recorded in the mid-19th century, an Ojibwa youth "heard the winds whistle, saw the tree waving its top, the earth heaving, heard the waters roaring, because they were all troubled and agitated." A manitou appeared to the boy, saying: "I am from the rising sun. I will come and see you again. You will not see me often." The boy's father subsequently interpreted his vision: "My son, the god of the winds is kind to you; the aged tree I hope may indicate long life; the wind may indicate that you will travel much; the water which you saw, and the winds, will carry your canoe safely through the waves."

In another vision, set down in the early 20th century, an Ojibwa recalled that on the fifth night of his fast he dreamed of a large, beautiful bird. He had already decided to reject his first vision, however, so he continued his quest. Three nights later, another bird appeared, and this one took him in his dream "to the north where there was only ice. There were very old birds there who promised me long life and health. I accepted and was brought back to my lodge." As the bird departed, the seeker recognized it as a white loon. For the rest of his life, therefore, that young man would have a special bond with the spirit of the white loon. This relationship would be hinted at, although perhaps not revealed, by the new name he adopted after his vision quest to replace the one that had been assigned him during his naming ceremony. And the loon would figure in the personal hymn he would sing thereafter, as well as in the picture he would draw on rock or tattoo on his body as a lifelong reminder of his vision.

Decorated with quills, this beaver medicine bundle was carried by a member of the Fox tribe. Such bundles held sacred items from which the owner drew strength in times of adversity.

After puberty, relationships beyond the immediate family became more important to the individual. The most significant of these ties was clan membership. Children in the lakes region were born into their father's clan (an exception being the Huron, who like the Iroquois followed the custom of joining the mother's clan). Like the individual, the clan had its own spiritual guardian—an ancestral manitou that bequeathed power to all future members. That spirit, known as the *dodem*, or "totem," was symbolized by a pictograph and celebrated in clan legends; in addition, a bundle of sacred objects relating to the guardian spirit was often kept in the lodge where clan members gathered for ceremonies. Most clans of the region traced their ancestry to the spirits of familiar and respected animals, such as the bear, the deer, the moose, and the eagle. But even dreaded creatures could inspire clans: The Winnebago had one devoted to the thunderbird and another devoted to the water monster.

The role of clans in the community varied from tribe to tribe. In no case could young people marry within their clan, a taboo that prevented incestuous alliances between descendants of the same spiritual ancestor and helped bring together members of different groups. Upon marriage, a young woman went to live with her husband and his kin, but she remained a member of her father's clan. By the mid-19th century, Ojibwa clans had few communal functions other than regulating matrimony, but tribal elders could remember a time when each major clan had a distinct character and responsibility. William Warren, the son of a white trader and an Ojibwa woman who chronicled the traditions of his mother's tribe, noted that members of the Bear Clan were said to resemble that animal in that they were "ill-tempered and fond of fighting." In the old days, he added, they were quick to challenge other tribes and often led the way in battle. According to Warren, many members of the Bear Clan, like their totem animal, boasted a "long, thick, coarse head of the blackest hair, which seldom becomes thin or white in old age."

At least two Ojibwa clans—the Loon and the Crane—prided themselves on providing the tribe with chiefs, and they sometimes quarreled as to which was foremost in that respect. Warren was present as interpreter in the early 1840s when leaders of the two clans met with an agent of the United States government on Madeline Island in Lake Superior—a site sacred to the Ojibwa. The head of the Loon Clan opened the council by proclaiming that his group had always occupied "first place and chieftainship among the Ojibwas." That assertion was then effectively rebutted by the head of the Crane Clan, a modest and retiring man, who arose and point-

ed toward the eastern skies. "The Great Spirit once made a bird," he related, "and he sent it from the skies to make its abode on earth. The bird came, and when it reached halfway down, among the clouds, it sent forth a loud and far sounding cry, which was heard by all who resided on the earth, and even by the spirits who make their abode within its bosom."

This heaven-sent crane alighted first by the rapids at Bawating, the speaker related, and raised a great cry that summoned to that place the bear, the marten, the moose, and the other totem animals of the Ojibwa who later congregated there. Then the crane took wing and flew westward over Lake Superior until it approached La Pointe on Madeline Island. Once again, the bird issued its cry. From the waters below, the loon re-

A prominent Ojibwa shaman named Shakopee (far right) wears traditional finery that sets him apart from the relatives standing outside his wigwam in contemporary dress in this late-19th-century photograph.

sponded with a call so pure and melodic that it sounded sweeter to the crane than his own voice. "Henceforth," he told the loon, "you will answer for me in council." So it was, the speaker concluded, that when the clan leaders of the Ojibwa assembled, the loon "became first in council, but he who made him chief was the crane." Few would argue with the speaker's point, Warren added, for the Loon Clan had a claim to leadership that extended back only as far as "their first intercourse with the old French discoverers and traders," while the preeminence of the Crane Clan was attested to in ancient tribal lore.

Other tribes of the region assigned specific responsibilities to various clans, as well. The Winnebago traditionally chose chiefs from the ranks of the Thunderbird Clan; indeed, the position often passed from father to son, assuming the son was considered worthy of the honor. Such chiefs were peacemakers, who resolved disputes within the community and tried to avoid provoking other tribes. When warfare was unavoidable, the Winnebago looked for guidance to a separate clan that was originally dedicated to the hawk but whose members became known simply as the warriors, or "fear-inspiring men." Like others in the region, the Winnebago believed that authority in peacetime should be distinct from leadership in wartime, although the peacetime chief might discourage a raid he disagreed with. Any warrior who announced his intention to mount an expedition—usually as a result of a vision directing him to avenge a death or increase his stature—could do so provided his reputation was sufficient to attract and hold enough followers. This was no small challenge, since each warrior was free to leave the party at any time. As one 18th-century observer noted, a war chief "has no other means of control over the individuals than his personal influence gives him."

When it came to policing Winnebago communities, the Bear Clan took the lead. If an individual tried to hunt where he was not supposed to or harvest wild rice that was meant for others, the vigilant Bear clansmen could burn his lodge. If the offender resisted, the enforcers were free to whip or even kill him, and his relatives had no recourse. The Bear clansmen, like the members of other Winnebago clans, expressed their solidarity by maintaining certain names for their exclusive use and conducting annual feasts and ceremonies.

Potentially, strong clan loyalties could divide a tribe into hostile factions. But lakes tribes guarded against excessive clannishness not only by requiring that young people marry outside the clan but also by grouping clans together into larger associations. The Winnebago and Menominee had two such groupings, one consisting of clans named for creatures who lived in the sky and the other of clans named for creatures who lived on earth or in the water. A youngster from one grouping was required to seek a mate from the other, which meant that every marriage brought the two halves of the tribe together. Matters were more complicated among the Potawatomi, who had as many as 40 clans, grouped into six associations. But the tribe divided itself neatly into two halves for ceremonial purposes by classifying children according to the order of their birth in the family, with the odd-numbered children belonging to the "senior side" and the even-numbered children to the "junior side." A village might break down along those lines to play a game of lacrosse, for example. For all the jostling between the two sides, the game celebrated the ties that bound the community together.

Although the clans and larger associations played an important part in the social and ceremonial life of the people, deeper spiritual concerns were addressed through personal rituals, through seasonal festivities involving the entire community, and through the observances of shamans and medicine societies. Individuals affirmed their devotion to their guardian manitou and to other spirits by singing songs, including the one derived from the vision quest, other personal songs inspired by dreams

A Potawatomi prescription stick (bottom) indicates which herbs a shaman must combine to treat specific illnesses. Shamans administered herbal remedies in medicine bowls like the Winnebago vessel below, made from maple wood.

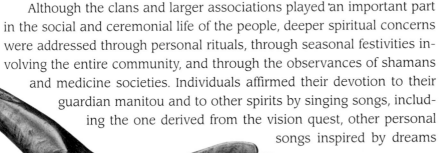

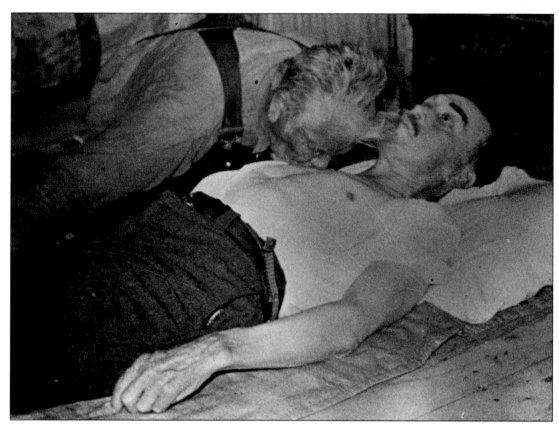

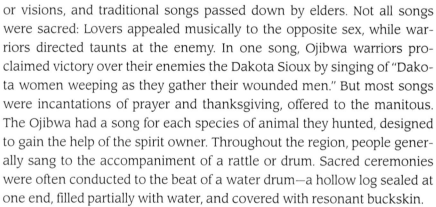

After praying for spiritual aid, an Ojibwa shaman known as a sucking doctor tries to draw the source of illness from his patient's chest. If a sucking doctor failed to remove the offending material, he appealed to another manitou and tried once more.

or visions, and traditional songs passed down by elders. Not all songs were sacred: Lovers appealed musically to the opposite sex, while warriors directed taunts at the enemy. In one song, Ojibwa warriors proclaimed victory over their enemies the Dakota Sioux by singing of "Dakota women weeping as they gather their wounded men." But most songs were incantations of prayer and thanksgiving, offered to the manitous. The Ojibwa had a song for each species of animal they hunted, designed to gain the help of the spirit owner. Throughout the region, people generally sang to the accompaniment of a rattle or drum. Sacred ceremonies were often conducted to the beat of a water drum—a hollow log sealed at one end, filled partially with water, and covered with resonant buckskin.

When singing or praying to a manitou, people sometimes reinforced their appeal with a gift. Typically, they offered tobacco, of which the manitous were said to be extremely fond. Land or water spirits were offered pinches of tobacco—tossed on stormy water, for example, to reinforce a request for calm. When gathering herbs or harvesting rice, people left some tobacco on the ground as a gesture of thanksgiving. Offerings to the sky manitous were made in the form of smoke. A traveler in need of good weather, for instance, lighted a pipe or threw tobacco into the fire and sent fragrant smoke to the four winds. Other prized substances, such as wild rice or certain herbs, were offered to influence the animal spirits, attract lovers, ensure good luck, or counteract evil influences. On special occasions, people honored the spirits by sacrificing one of the dogs that roamed their camps as scavengers. The supreme offering was a white dog, which the Ojibwa sacrificed to the sun and the moon at a rite held each autumn.

Although only the spirits and the shamans who were able to commune with them could influence events, many ordinary people knew of ways to foresee the future or discern things that were hidden. One technique, scrying, involved staring into clear water or some other smooth surface until a trancelike state ensued, during which revelations occurred as to the location of game, enemies, or lost objects. Another method used to locate game involved placing an animal's shoulder blade or some other bone near a fire so that cracks formed in a pattern that could then be deciphered. Simply rolling a handful of stones across smooth ground, it was thought, offered clues as to the whereabouts of a war party.

When people wanted to give thanks for blessings that came with the seasons and ensure that those blessings would recur in years to come, they gathered for one of the communal observances that marked their annual round. Feasts honoring the spirits were held when the maple sap began to run, when the first berries were ready for picking, and when the

Ojibwas erected this pole framework for a shaking-tent doctor, who communed with spirits inside the tent to help people who were sick or troubled. The lower part of the structure was covered during the ceremony to shield the doctor from view.

This effigy with a chest cavity containing a variety of charms belonged to an Ojibwa shaman. Some shamans treated patients by transferring their illness to an effigy, which was then symbolically killed.

wild rice had been harvested, among other occasions. Family groups paid homage to the spirit of the bear at their camps in midwinter, and sometime during the year, each individual was expected to host a feast to his guardian manitou.

One spiritual concern that knew no season was the desire to fend off sickness and other dire misfortunes. For that purpose, the lakes people resorted to individuals who were thought to have acquired special power, or medicine, from the spirits. These shamans were not exclusively concerned with curing people, but in one way or another, they all worked to restore balance and well-being to the world. In some cases, they were called upon to reverse the harm done by witches or sorcerers, who claimed power from the spirits as well but used it maliciously. Other disturbances that shamans dealt with were said to be caused by frustrated hopes and longings within the patient, or by manitous offended by some deliberate or accidental slight. There were so many possible sources of illness that only a shaman could divine the cause and prescribe a cure with any confidence.

Typically, every extended family included at least one shaman, whose powers were not necessarily of the highest order but who was readily consulted by his or her relatives. In some cases, shamans were inspired at an early age by manitous that others might recoil from. "When I was a boy of six, I was always dreaming about snakes," one Ojibwa shaman recalled. Subsequently, in his defining vision quest, a voice told him to strip and sit under an oak tree: "Two snakes came near, then more, and more, and pretty soon they were crawling all over me—you couldn't see my skin. After a while, they left except for two around the front of my middle, who stayed with their heads nearly meeting. I heard a voice say, 'You will have this till you die.' So these are my manitous." For an ordinary person, an encounter with snake spirits might be considered ominous, but this youth was blessed with the ability to put the potent medicine of such manitous to good use. Even youngsters granted the most inspiring visions, however, remained apprentices until they were mature enough to exert that awesome power.

One class of shaman known as the *wabeno* was adept at herbal remedies in particular. Tribes around the Great Lakes were familiar with the uses of some 400 plants and herbs in treating illness. Everyone knew how to prepare herbal teas and potions and use them to relieve aches, pains, digestive upsets, fainting spells, and respiratory ailments. But wabenos had access to special remedies that they had learned from elders during their apprenticeship or from the manitous during dreams and visions. Wabenos sometimes demonstrated their powers at feasts and dances by handling burning coals and red-hot stones, having first applied herbal ointments to their hands. Early French observers referred to them and their fellow shamans as *jongleurs,* or "jugglers," and made light of their ceremonies. But at least one Frenchman conceded that the shamans had strong medicine at their disposal, including an herbal remedy that proved an effective antidote to snake venom.

There were other kinds of healing shamans. One was the seer, who looked for agents of illness within the patient and tried to suck them out through a tube. The seer, or sucking doctor, treated maladies that were thought to enter the body in the form of tiny objects, such as a worm or a sliver of stone or wood. Removing them required keen spiritual insight, and the shaman began the ceremony by paying tribute to his patron manitou. "When a sucking doctor starts to cure," recalled Tom Badger, who in his youth was treated by such a shaman for a severe pain in his side, "he first tells the people there

about the dream he had at the time he was fasting." Having invoked his guardian manitou, the shaman would then shake his medicine rattle and set out his implements—two small, hollow bones, which he placed in a dish of water and proceeded to pick up with his mouth. Tom Badger's doctor had so much power that when he "leaned over the dish, the bones stood up and moved toward his mouth. He swallowed the bones twice and coughed them up again."

Then the shaman pressed one of the tubes hard against the patient's side, broke the skin, and sucked out the offending object along with blood, which he first emptied into a dish and then cast into the fire. In this instance, the harmful object was too small to be detected amid the blood by the patient, but others reported seeing worms or fragments of stone in the matter extracted from them by shamans. This operation was not enough in itself to cure the patient; in order to keep the malady from recurring, the seer was required to identify the root cause. In Tom Badger's case, the shaman pronounced, the underlying problem was a thwarted wish. At a medicine dance some time before, Tom Badger had been presented with a hide that his father subsequently gave to someone else. "You promised to give him another one," the shaman reminded the boy's father. "Sometimes he thinks about it. That is why he is sick now."

Perhaps the most impressive healing rite practiced by the Great Lakes Indians was the shaking-tent ceremony, presided over by a shaman the Ojibwa called a *djiskiu,* or "shaking-tent doctor." This powerful medicine man might invoke the aid of the spirits to cure a single patient or to help an entire community afflicted by plague, famine, or some other dire misfortune. When appealed to, the shaking-tent doctor would first take a sweat bath to purify himself and then supervise the building of a tent for the ceremony. This was a small, cylindrical structure framed by a circle of poles and covered with hides or birch bark. The tent was open at the top, so that those in attendance could hear but not see the shaman. Come sunset, the relatives of the sick person or members of the endangered community would gather around this tent, and the shaking-tent doctor would approach, singing to let the manitous know that he wanted to see them and that they should enter the tent at the same time he did.

Canadian anthropologist Diamond Jenness, who spent time among the Ojibwas on Parry Island in 1929, evoked the drama of the shaking-tent doctor at work: "At last he approaches, crawls beneath the birch-bark en-

As demonstrated at left by a Winnebago scribe, Great Lakes Indians recorded their history and lore in pictographs on birch-bark scrolls like the one above, which conveys sacred teachings of the lakes tribes' Midewiwin, or Grand Medicine Society.

velope, and disappears within. He is speaking. We cannot distinguish the words, but we know he is calling the *manido* [manitou] that blessed him during his puberty fast, and the other manidos that always lend their aid. There is a sudden thud, and the lodge rocks violently, for a spirit *(medewadji:* a spirit of the ceremonial lodge) has entered it. Another thud and further rocking; then another, and still another. . . . Inside the lodge there are now five or six medewadji or manidos, souls or spirits of animals like the bear and the serpent, who have assembled together with the spirit of thunder, and of snapping turtle, longest lived of all creatures, their interpreter. We cannot see them, but we understand that turtle rests at the bottom of the lodge, feet up, keeping it from sinking into the ground; that thunder is at the top, covering it like a lid; and that the other spirits are perched around the hoop that encircles the frame."

The people in attendance, Jenness added, could hear the various spirits conferring in high-pitched voices as to the cause of the disturbance and the appropriate cure. Sometimes the manitous blamed a sorcerer and promised to punish him if he did not take back the harm he had done. Sometimes, they lent the ailing person the soul of a healthy one, who himself became ill for a time but soon recovered. On rare occasions, they concluded that there was no remedy. One Ojibwa remembered attending a shaking-tent ceremony held for a gravely ill child: "We heard the manidos say to one another inside the lodge: 'We cannot do anything. The child will have to die.' " And so it happened.

True shaking-tent doctors were possessed by the spirits they summoned and never sought to contrive effects. Near the end of his life, a former shaman who had converted to Christianity was asked if the manifestations of his shaking-tent ceremonies had been mere tricks. "I cannot live much longer, and I can do no other than speak the truth," he responded. "I did not deceive you at that time. I did not move the lodge. It was shaken by the power of the spirits. Nor did I speak to you with a double tongue, I only

A 19th-century Ottawa drawing shows participants in a Midewiwin Great Medicine Dance holding sacred objects, including smoking pipes, a bow, a drum, and a medicine pouch, which was presented to society initiates during the ceremony. The beating of the drum summoned manitous to the dance.

Winnebago initiates carrying decorated medicine pouches made of beaver fur leave a Midewiwin lodge after the end of a Great Medicine Dance in 1896.

repeated to you what the spirits said to me. I heard their voices. The top of the lodge was filled with them, and before me the sky and the wide lands lay expanded." So great was the power of the spirits they dealt with that shaking-tent doctors risked exhaustion if they summoned them too frequently. Many such shamans had knowledge of herbal remedies and dispensed them as often as they were requested, but they seldom performed a shaking-tent ceremony more than once a month for fear of overburdening their soul and losing their gift.

The deep concern of the people of the lakes for maintaining a proper ceremonial relationship with the spirits led to the development—first among the Ojibwa and later among neighboring tribes—of the Grand Medicine Society, or Midewiwin (a term that translates loosely as "things done to the sound of the drum"). This society, which still functions today, has long devoted itself not only to curing rituals but also to other ancestral traditions relating to the manitous and their powers. It was the Midewiwin who elaborated the accounts of the Anishinabe and their westward journey from the great salt sea, guided by the sacred Megis. And Mide storytellers such as Tom Badger preserved and passed along many of the richest and fullest accounts of Wenebojo and his feats. But the overriding

purpose of the society was to perform ceremonies designed to instill in each new generation of initiates the powers that had been bequeathed to their predecessors by the spirits.

Perhaps to compete more effectively with the Jesuits and other fervent missionary groups who sought to convert Indians of the region to Christianity, the Grand Medicine Society imposed strict order and discipline on its membership. Initiates were required to act honorably at all times and renounce the use of alcohol. And each member was assigned a rank within a Mide hierarchy consisting of several orders, or degrees. Acceptance into even the lowest degree of the society required lengthy instruction, for which substantial fees had to be paid. One visitor in 1860 noted that an Ojibwa acquaintance had paid for his Mide instruction in furs that would have earned him a small fortune from traders. Initiates learned their lessons by pondering the stories told by society members and by studying

Ceremonially dressed and painted for his journey to the next world and clasping a pipe tomahawk in his left hand, an Ojibwa chief named Flat Mouth is laid out for burial at Leech Lake, Minnesota, in 1907.

birch-bark scrolls inscribed with pictographs that concerned the creation of the world, the migration of the Anishinabe, sacred songs and prayers, and other religious matters. The scrolls were regarded not simply as aids for memorizing the traditions of the society but as messages from the spirits, imbued with their power. As one Mide leader said of the scrolls, "When the manitou spoke to the Indians, he told them to worship according to this parchment."

Candidates were initiated into the society during an elaborate ceremony known as the Great Medicine Dance, which was held once or twice a year in late spring or early fall. This rite, consisting of eight parts and extending over several days, was also the occasion for promoting existing members to higher ranks (traditionally, there were eight levels of rank in the society, the lower four being earth degrees and the higher four, sky degrees). The highlight of the Great Medicine Dance was the initiation ceremony, during which the candidates for admission were symbolically killed and then brought back to life. Some candidates had recently experienced a serious illness; others were healthy but had been instructed in a dream or vision to undergo this symbolic ordeal so that they might be fortified with protective spirit power.

At a special lodge constructed for the occasion, the candidates' sponsors joined in a dance. At the climax of the ritual, sponsors pointed their medicine bags at the candidates and pretended to shoot them by tossing cowrie shells at their feet. The candidates pretended they had been pierced by the cowries and fell to the ground as if dead, whereupon the shells were removed and the candidates were revived and presented with their own medicine bags, filled with herbal remedies and sacred objects that would keep them well. The cowries shot at the candidates represented the sacred sign, or Megis, that guided the Anishinabe on their westward journey from the great salt sea. Much as that shell lured the Anishinabe away from their old life and introduced them to a new one, the shooting of the cowries brought to a close one existence for the candidate and marked the beginning of another. This miraculous moment of death and renewal was celebrated in an initiation song of the Midewiwin:

> *The shell goes toward them*
> *And they fall.*
> *My Mide brother is searched.*
> *In his heart is found*
> *That which I seek to remove:*
> *A white shell*

There was no ceremony, however powerful, that could forestall the inevitable afflictions of old age. Indeed, individuals who lived unusually long lives were regarded by the people of the lakes with some ambivalence. On the one hand, such elders might well have survived because they had earned the blessing of benevolent spirits. On the other hand, they might be in touch with evil powers.

The Winnebago believed, for example, that witches often killed people in order to claim the victim's remaining years of life, in which case advanced age might indicate skill in sorcery. Few people cared to live so long that they became a burden to their neighbors and kin. Once the body grew feeble, death was welcome, for then the soul was free to travel outward, as it did for brief periods when one was dreaming.

The purpose of funeral rites among the lakes Indians was to speed the

In a painting depicting an actual funeral near Kewanna, Indiana, in 1837, the brother of a deceased Potawatomi girl leads her pallbearers and a cortege of mourners to a tribal burial place.

In a work by the same artist, women bid farewell to the departed girl, sprinkling handfuls of soil onto the coffin. Funeral rites were vital to ensure a safe journey for the deceased down the "road of souls."

soul on its way to the next world, which lay in the direction of the setting sun. Family members typically laid out the deceased in the wigwam on a sheet of birch bark, after combing and braiding the hair, painting the face, and arraying the body in the finest clothing and surrounding it with treasured possessions and equipment. With family and friends assembled, a shaman or Mide leader gave the soul of the deceased advice about avoiding evil spirits on its westward journey. The soul might be warned of the great obstacle that lay ahead—a rushing river, spanned by a quaking log, or rolling bridge, which was really a dreaded underwater manitou in the

form of a snake. In order to pass safely over, the soul would have to speak respectfully to the manitou and make an offering of tobacco.

It was the mourners' duty to provide the soul with food and tobacco for this journey. Menominee warriors called on enemies they had killed in battle to escort their relative to the afterworld. Speakers made it clear that they expected the soul to depart immediately, without hanging back to disturb the living or coax someone else along to the next world. "You will see your dead relatives," one funeral speech went. "They will inquire about the people still living. Tell them we are not ready to come." One French visitor among the Ottawa observed that relatives gathered around the lodge of their dead kinsman in the evening and made dreadful noises to encourage the soul to take flight and "go and see their ancestors."

After sending the soul on its way, the family removed the body from the wigwam through a hole cut in the west wall, opposite the eastward-facing entrance. The body was never taken out by the entrance, for fear that the shadow—an elusive element of the personality that lingered after death as a ghost—might one day return that same way to haunt the inhabitants. The relatives then laid the body and its possessions, wrapped in birch bark, in a shallow grave. They marked the grave with a stake bearing an inverted symbol of the deceased's clan totem, and perhaps other pictographs recording the person's special qualities and achievements. Relatives placed food near the grave as symbolic nourishment for the journeying soul, and every evening for four nights kindled a fire nearby to warm the soul when it rested at night.

After four days, it was said, the soul reached the river and paid tribute to the dreaded manitou that offered the only path to the other side. Once the soul crossed over, it neared its long-sought goal. As the French explorer and interpreter Nicolas Perrot described the afterlife envisioned by the people of the Great Lakes region, souls on the far side of the river "enter a delightful country, in which excellent fruits are found in abundance." Just ahead, he added, the souls can see kindred spirits dancing to the beat of drums and the rattling of gourds. The nearer the travelers approach, the louder grows the music, and the greater the excitement of the dancers. Soon the souls reach the "place where the dance is held, and are cordially received by all." The dancers offer the newcomers refreshment, inviting them to feast to their heart's delight. Then at last, the souls are ready to join in the great celebration: "They go to mingle with the others—to dance and make merry forever, without being any longer subject to sorrow, anxiety, or infirmities, or to any of the vicissitudes of mortal life." ◆

Crosses rise amid Ojibwa burial houses at a Christian church on Minnesota's Grand Portage Reservation in 1885. Relatives honored the deceased by leaving offerings of berries or maple sugar outside the burial house.

This photograph from the early 20th century shows a Midewiwin medicine man dressed in ceremonial garb decorated with secret symbols relating to the society's rituals.

The split feathers of this beaded Midewiwin headdress indicate that it was reserved for ritual use.

THE POWER OF THE MIDEWIWIN

For the Ojibwa as for other Native American tribes, contact with Europeans threatened traditional institutions and beliefs. To help maintain the old ways and ward off the evil effects of changes brought by the whites, the Ojibwa relied on the rituals and practices of the ancient religious society that they called Midewiwin. As the society's ceremonies evolved over the centuries, they grew increasingly complex, combining elements of the Ojibwa creation myth, the traditional vision quest, herbal medicine for promoting and ensuring good health, and ritual healing.

Each year, the Great Medicine Dance of the Midewiwin united the community through an elaborate series of ceremonies. These rituals were conducted by an exclusive hierarchy of experienced men and women—distinguished by their knowledge and healing powers. Using the secret instructions that were recorded as symbols on birch-bark scrolls, the Mide masters initiated new and existing members into one of several successive degrees of secret wisdom. It was also a time for ailing members of the community to present themselves to be healed with the help of the Midewiwin.

Before the Great Medicine Dance ceremony, blankets presented to Midewiwin elders by candidates for various levels of the society are hung from the center pole of the medicine lodge.

In the uncovered medicine lodge, a mother holds her child as Mide elders file past. Although most participants in the ceremony were initiates or members of the society, some were sick or anticipated illness. Performing cures was one way a member could advance to the next degree in the society.

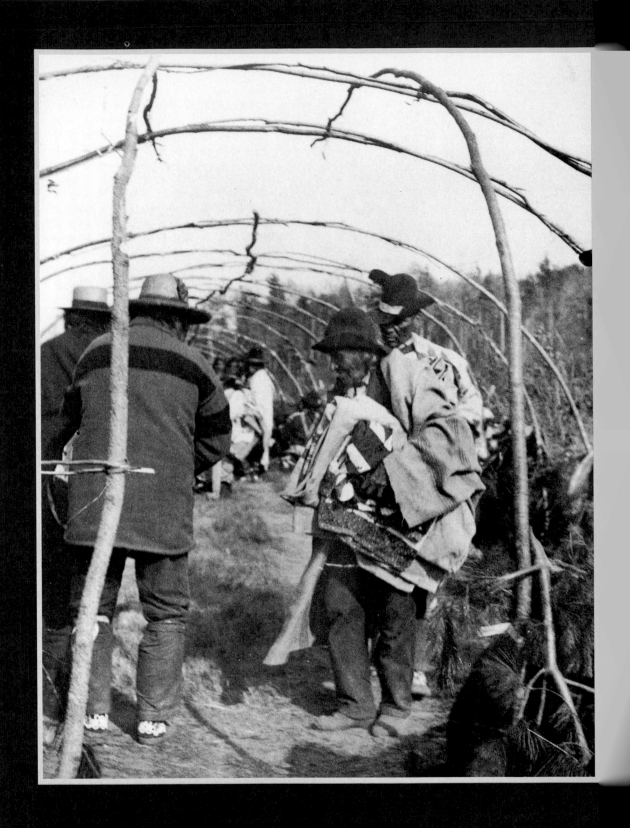

Women Midewiwin await the distribution of the medicine bundles hanging from lodge poles. Such bundles were presented to candidates at the completion of each degree. They were to be filled with objects possessing healing powers for use at future Midewiwin ceremonies. A medicine bag of beaver skin (right) was presented at the completion of the first degree.

THE ART OF WOMEN'S WORK

In the tradition of the Indians of the Great Lakes, the women were responsible not only for making their family's clothes but also for decorating them so that their beauty would please the myriad spirits abiding in the natural world. The products of especially skilled craftswomen, however, came to have economic as well as spiritual worth. Fine finished garments and accessories became valuable barter items, first in intertribal trade and then in the fur trade. When a cash economy was later imposed on the Indians, the women's creations offered a means of acquiring money.

Intricate floral bead-work adorns this Ojibwa tablecloth, a dazzling example of the work that Great Lakes Indian women—such as the one shown sewing below—have created for centuries.

Among the most ancient decorative arts practiced by Indian women of the Great Lakes region were quill-work, moose-hair embroidery, and weaving. In quill-work, the quills of the porcupine were dyed with pigments made from plants and then appliquéd onto leather garments, bags, and moccasins in ornamental designs. Huron women excelled at moose-hair embroidery, applying the dyed hair to birch bark, deerskin, or cloth. The ancient practice of wrapping the hair around materials was modernized in the early 17th century, when Ursuline nuns in Quebec taught Indian girls to embroider using needles.

Weaving involved finger braiding nettle fibers or the stringy insides of tree bark into sashes and bags. By 1800 Indian weavers were also using wool yarn obtained through trade with Europeans.

By the turn of the 19th century, Great Lakes women had integrated two new imports—glass beads and silk ribbons—into their art. Beadwork and ribbonwork often echoed the rich patterns found in traditional quillwork and weaving. Eventually the artisans began employing European-style floral imagery in their beadwork and creating objects—such as the tablecloth above—to appeal to European and American tastes. A sampler of the extraordinary artistry of the Great Lakes Indian craftswomen appears on the following pages.

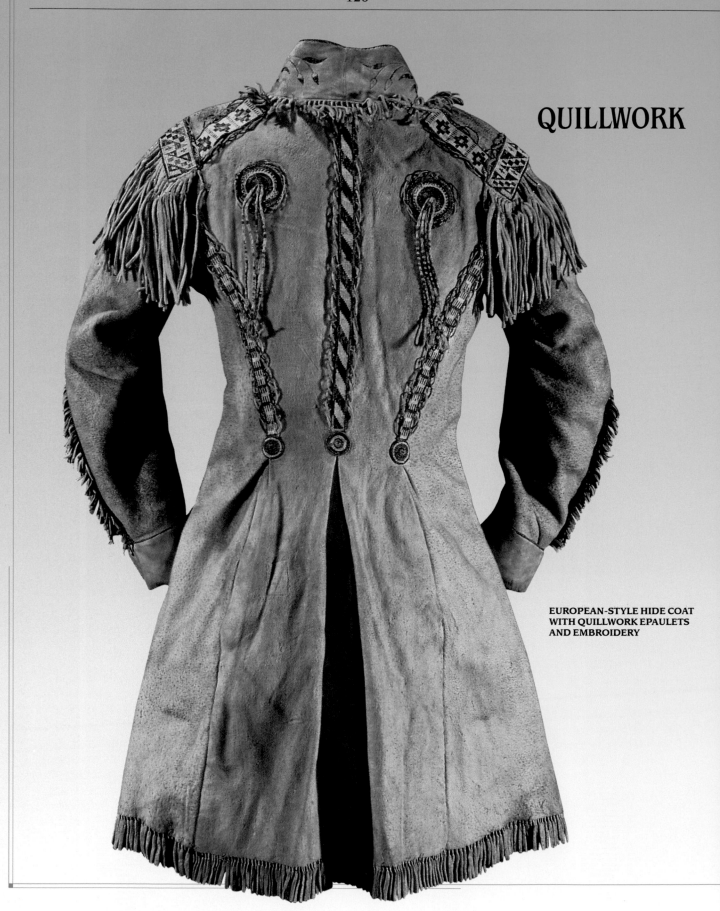

QUILLWORK

**EUROPEAN-STYLE HIDE COAT
WITH QUILLWORK EPAULETS
AND EMBROIDERY**

QUILLED MENOMINEE KNIFE
CASE OF BLACKENED BUCKSKIN

OTTAWA BUCKSKIN POUCH WITH
QUILLWORK AND GLASS BEADS

WINNEBAGO OTTER-SKIN BAG WITH
QUILLWORK AND SILK RIBBON

MOOSE-HAIR EMBROIDERY

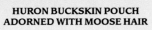

**HURON BUCKSKIN POUCH
ADORNED WITH MOOSE HAIR**

**HURON BUCKSKIN MOCCASIN
EMBROIDERED WITH MOOSE HAIR**

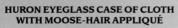

**HURON EYEGLASS CASE OF CLOTH
WITH MOOSE-HAIR APPLIQUÉ**

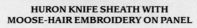

**HURON KNIFE SHEATH WITH
MOOSE-HAIR EMBROIDERY ON PANEL**

HURON BURDEN STRAP OF INDIAN HEMP WITH MOOSE HAIR AND GLASS BEADS

WEAVING

**FOX SASH OF WOOL YARN
WITH GLASS BEADS**

POTAWATOMI BAG OF COTTON
TWINE AND WOOL YARN

FOX CHARM BAG OF WOOL YARN

GREAT LAKES ARMBAND OF BRAIDED WOOL YARN

BEADWORK

WINNEBAGO MAN'S WOOL SHIRT WITH GLASS BEADS AND SILK AND VELVET RIBBON

OJIBWA CLOTH SHOULDER BAG WITH GLASS BEADS

MENOMINEE MAN'S DECORATIVE GARTER WITH BEADED LEAF DESIGN

FOX BEAR-CLAW NECKLACE WITH OTTER PELT, GRIZZLY CLAWS, AND GLASS BEADS

RIBBONWORK

**OJIBWA WOOLEN HOOD WITH
SILK RIBBON AND GLASS BEADS**

**OJIBWA CLOTH SHOULDER BAG WITH SILK
RIBBON AND GLASS AND METALLIC BEADS**

**POTAWATOMI WOOLEN WEARING
BLANKET WITH SILK RIBBON**

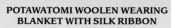

**POTAWATOMI BUCKSKIN MOCCASIN WITH
SILK RIBBON AND GLASS BEADS**

3

THE CURSE OF THE FUR TRADE

Faced with an 1837 treaty forcing the Winnebago to leave their native Wisconsin, Chiefs Black-hawk (left) and Winneshiek resisted, leading a band of followers who refused to relocate. The group remained in their homeland—as fugitives—for more than 25 years.

One day in 1634, a canoe bearing seven Indian guides and a single Frenchman scraped ashore at what is now Green Bay, in the northwest corner of Lake Michigan. This small party had much to fear, for the bay and its environs were then home to the Winnebago, a populous Siouan-speaking people who resisted any dealings with foreigners and their Indian trading partners. On one occasion, a French official later reported, Ottawa emissaries had approached the Winnebago and tried to persuade them to join the Ottawa in trading with the pale-skinned strangers from the east, who sought furs from the people of the lakes and offered in return wondrous implements of metal as well as glass beads and cloth. Perhaps the Winnebago feared that the mysterious white men and their wares were evil medicine. In any case, their response was uncompromising. They seized the Ottawas as enemies, executed them, and ate their flesh in ritual fashion.

The seven Indians who came ashore at Green Bay might have suffered a similar fate had they ventured there alone. But the Frenchman accompanying them impressed the Winnebagos. He wore a heavy, shimmering cloak embroidered with birds and flowers—only a man in touch with powerful spirits would be so grandly attired. He brought with him fire sticks: magical weapons that smoked and thundered. And although he seemed to come from another world, he conversed fluently in a language akin to that of the Winnebagos' Algonquian-speaking neighbors.

This gifted speaker was Jean Nicolet, an aide to the celebrated French officer and explorer Samuel de Champlain, who had helped found the colony of New France in what is now the province of Quebec. Nicolet had been sent as a boy to grow up among the Algonquian-speaking Nipissing, who lived around the lake of that name, northeast of Georgian Bay. As a part of their colonial endeavors, the French made a point of immersing themselves in native cultures, and Nicolet had so adapted himself to the Nipissing lifeways that, as a colleague wrote, "he could have passed for one of that nation." Now, he was on a vital mission for Champlain. He was to explore to the west, not only to appease the Winnebago but also to seek

a route to the fabled resources of the Orient, which some thought lay just beyond the vast inland lakes. That was why he brought with him the magnificent embroidered robe. He meant to impress Oriental potentates, if he succeeded in reaching their country.

That goal was unattainable, but Nicolet's parley with the Winnebagos helped open the western lakes region to France and her British successors in the area. Before he and the Indians accompanying him returned eastward, Nicolet had enticed the reluctant Winnebagos to join in a fur trade that would have far-reaching consequences for all the people of the lakes. For now, the prospects seemed as dazzling to them as Nicolet's robe. But as time passed, many native peoples who dealt with the whites would recall old warnings about the intruders. Among the Ojibwa, it was said, a prophet had foretold that "the white spirits would come in numbers like sand on the lakeshore, and would sweep the red race from the hunting grounds, which the Great Spirit had given them as an inheritance." For the descendants of the Anishinabe, the prophet insisted, the coming of the white man would mean the end of their world.

A 1743 sketch by Hudson's Bay trader James Isham meticulously details various beaver-hunting techniques in an effort to satisfy European curiosity. A closer look at the coveted animal (above) appeared in the journal of French officer Baron de Lahontan in 1703.

The vast lake country extending westward from the villages that were occupied by the Ottawa and the Huron around Georgian Bay to the headwaters of the Mississippi River supported a host of fur-bearing animals prized in Europe for their pelts, including mink and ermine, fox, marten, and otter. It was the beaver, however, that preoccupied fur traders in North America. For the pelt of that industrious rodent proved to be the ideal material from which to manufacture the felt hats that were in such demand among Europeans. By the mid-18th century, hundreds of thousands of beaver pelts were making their way each year from North America to factories located in France, England, and other European nations. In the process, the forests of the Northeast were all but depopulated of beaver, and traders seeking the furs pressed farther westward into the woodlands around the Great Lakes.

The fur trade, it turned out, would deplete not only the beaver but also the tribes that provided the pelts. Along with foreign goods, the intruders brought diseases against which the Indians had no immunity. The resulting epidemics were just the first in a series of traumas to beset the people of the lakes. Many generations of conflict and upheaval lay ahead, as tribes first vied with one another for an edge in the fur trade and later became swept up in punishing struggles between European powers for control of the region and its assets.

By the time Jean Nicolet arrived at Green Bay to confer with the Winnebagos, epidemics were already taking their toll around the eastern Great Lakes, where many Indians were in close contact with whites. Smallpox was the greatest killer, with measles, scarlet fever, diphtheria, typhus, whooping cough, and influenza all claiming their share. The Huron—who allowed Jesuit missionaries to reside at their villages around the lower end of Georgian Bay in order to preserve their strong trading relationship with the French—were among the first to be devastated. By 1638 a Huron population that had exceeded 20,000 when Frenchmen first appeared in the region had been reduced to little more than 12,000. By the following year, the Ottawa to the north were in the grip of a massive smallpox epidemic. Soon the devastation swept westward, as French traders and missionaries advanced across the region, accompanied by Indian guides from tribes already affected.

Aside from claiming countless lives, the fur trade and the epidemics it unleashed set the stage for deadly tribal warfare. One early struggle pitted the Huron against their old enemies, the Iroquois of the Five Nations. Although the Iroquois suffered no less from European-borne diseases than did the Huron, they maintained their aggressive posture, thanks in part to the willingness of their Dutch trading partners along the Hudson River to ply them with muskets and gunpowder in exchange for beaver pelts. The French, by contrast, offered firearms only to the Hurons they trusted and spurned the others—the traditionalists who opposed the black-robed Jesuits and their countrymen. The divided Hurons fell prey to Iroquois attacks in the late 1640s that destroyed several fortified villages and panicked surrounding communities. Some Christian Hurons went east with the French and settled near Quebec; others sought refuge with neighboring tribes, including the Iroquoian-speaking Petun; still others were rounded up by the Iroquois and carried home as captives to the Five Nations, where most were adopted to help replenish the Iroquois population.

After dispersing the Huron, Iroquois war parties set out against other tribes, bent on seizing captives and furs. By 1651 the Iroquois had overrun southwestern Ontario, dislodging the Ottawa and scattering the Petun along with the Hurons they were harboring. Those Hurons who were not killed or captured fled farther west and became known to the people of the lakes by their ancestral name of Wendat (the British later referred to them as the Wyandot). Over the next few years, Iroquois warriors continued their destructive raids, sweeping across southern Michigan and northern Indiana and ousting the Potawatomi and the Miami. The attackers had no interest in occupying territory and regularly returned to their home villages, laden with prisoners, pelts, and other booty. The mere approach of a large, well-armed Iroquois war party, however, was frequently enough to disperse tribes that as yet possessed few firearms and had been sorely afflicted by disease.

From all points of conflict, the refugees streamed north and west, many by canoe, others struggling overland through the forests, with hunger their constant companion. Refugee centers sprang up at places removed from the main thrust of the

In an 18th-century French drawing, a stylized Iroquois warrior wields an ax and traditional war club like the one pictured above. Beautifully crafted into the shape of an animal head, this formidable weapon of wood and iron could split a skull in a single blow.

Warriors arrive by boat and set fire to enemy longhouses in a 1575 French engraving depicting intertribal warfare along the Saint Lawrence River. Such traditional rivalries were intensified once the European fur trade grew to dominate Indian relations.

Iroquois raids, such as the Indian town of Bawating, or Sault Sainte Marie, where Nipissings and others from around the northern end of Lake Huron joined the ranks of the resident branch of Ojibwas known as Saulteurs; and Chequamegon Bay, at the western end of Lake Superior, where some Ottawas and Petuns found shelter near Ojibwa settlements such as La Pointe. But no sanctuary attracted a larger and more varied assortment of refugees than Green Bay, where Winnebagos had greeted Jean Nicolet and his party in 1634. By 1650 the original population of that site had dwindled. After inaugurating trade with the French, the Winnebago had been devastated by disease and further depleted when 500 of their warriors

Indians portaging and paddling canoes are part of the natural landscape in a 1676 French map of the Saint Lawrence Valley and Great Lakes region. Also depicted is the region's abundance of wildlife, including bear, deer, and the all-important beaver.

perished in a sudden storm after setting out in canoes to raid members of the Fox tribe who had recently settled in the area. The weakened Winnebago could do little to resist the flood of refugees to the area—perhaps 10,000 Indians from more than a half-dozen tribes, including Potawatomis, Miamis, and Mascoutens, a branch of the Ojibwa.

Soon the far-ranging Iroquois appeared at Green Bay, too, evidently in the hope of tapping new fur sources west of Lake Michigan. But they were far from home and short of provisions. In 1655 a large Iroquois war party approached the Potawatomi encampment of Mitchigami along Green Bay and requested provisions from the very people they were about to assault. It was a cynical appeal to the native tradition of hospitality, and the Potawatomis responded in kind by offering them food that had been laced with poison. The Iroquois discovered the trick in time, but they lacked the strength to retaliate. Instead, they split into two groups and retreated. Both parties were later set upon and slaughtered, one as it headed south into lands held by the Illinois, the other when it ran afoul of Saulteur warriors at the rapids near their home.

Several years later, in 1662, those same determined Saulteurs, joined by various allies, ambushed an Iroquois war party on a point of land jutting out into Whitefish Bay, west of Sault Sainte Marie. The attackers struck at dawn, armed not only with bows and clubs but also with muskets. Overwhelming the opposing camp, the Saulteurs and their cohorts wiped out the Nadoway, or Big Serpents, as the people of the lakes referred to the Iroquois, likening them to creatures long associated with death and destruction.

Such resistance helped induce the Iroquois to strike a temporary truce with the French and their Indian allies in 1667. The Iroquois attacks had never succeeded in choking off the French fur trade, and it now accelerated rapidly, with Ottawa and Potawatomi hunters and trappers visiting Montreal regularly. The peace also saw the beginnings of a movement by displaced peoples who were seeking to reclaim their ancestral homelands east of Lake Michigan, or at least to establish themselves in places that were favorable to their old lifeways. In 1671 Ottawas and Petuns left Chequamegon Bay and moved east to the Straits of Mackinac, between Lakes Michigan and Huron; they settled at present-day Saint Ignace, then known as Michilimackinac. By the late 1680s, Potawatomis and Miamis were leaving their Green Bay sanctuaries and traveling down along the western and southern shores of Lake Michigan to raise new villages in or near their ancestral territories.

Some native groups settled near Jesuit missions located at trading centers. The sight of the first black-robed Jesuits who accompanied fur traders on their visits and stepped ashore with the cross held high above their heads so impressed Ojibwas that they came to refer to the French collectively as Wemitigoji, or Wavers of Wooden Sticks. Nonetheless, the Black Robes encountered resistance. Indians of the region tended to blame their maladies on the work of witches, and they had reason to wonder if the priests were not somehow responsible for the ills plaguing their villages. After all, the priests were reclusive beings who had no wives or families, did not give feasts, and sometimes defied respected elders and medicine men. In time, missionaries overcame some of this hostility and claimed more than a few converts. But critics of their efforts such as the French officer Baron de Lahontan contended that the only Indians willing to submit were those "on the point of death." Overall, the early missionaries made little headway with the people of the lakes.

In the 1680s, the Iroquois resumed their westward raids, encouraged by their recent covenant with the English, who had supplanted the Dutch along the Hudson River and emerged as formidable colonial rivals to the French. In the developing conflict, however, the English left the Iroquois largely to their own devices. By contrast, French troops sometimes fought alongside the embattled tribes of the lakes.

Although the Big Serpents no longer struck terror in the hearts of the Ojibwa and their northern neighbors, Iroquois war parties succeeded in intimidating other tribes to the south. In 1680 they swept down with such ferocity on the Illinois who were living below Lake Michigan that many bands of that tribe fled westward across the Mississippi River. One group of Illinois known as the Tamaroas made a brave stand—only to be crushed in a battle that left 700 of them captured or killed. In years to come, however, the tide turned against the Iroquois. By the late 1680s, Indians with French support were mounting retaliatory raids deep into Iroquois territory. The conflict had come full circle.

Despite such military success, the people of the lakes were not always

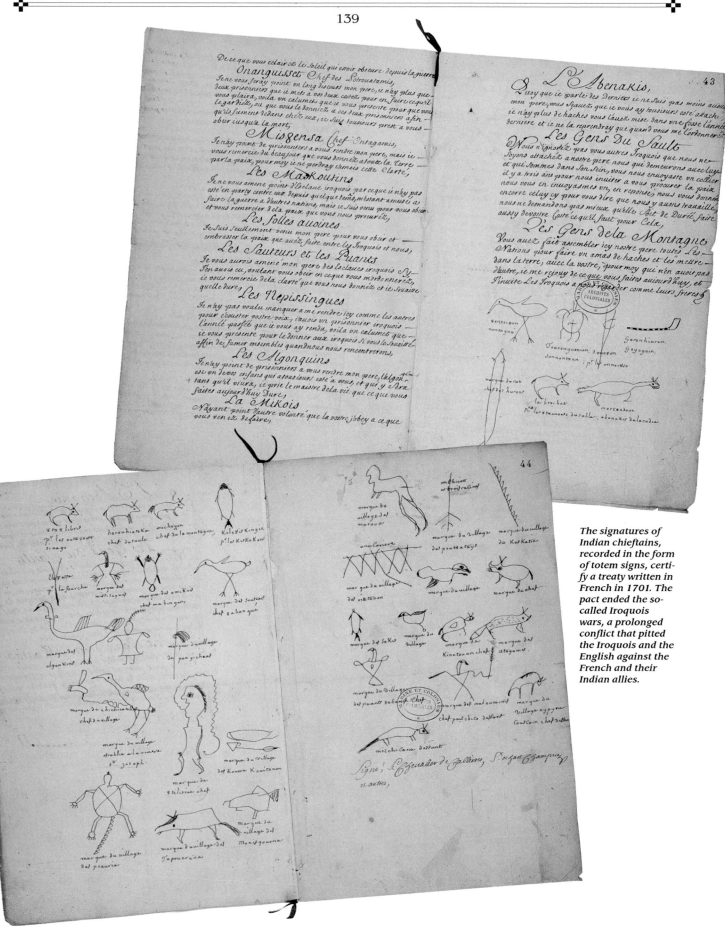

The signatures of Indian chieftains, recorded in the form of totem signs, certify a treaty written in French in 1701. The pact ended the so-called Iroquois wars, a prolonged conflict that pitted the Iroquois and the English against the French and their Indian allies.

content with their French allies. Fearful of English competition, the French began fortifying their trading posts around the Great Lakes and asserting dominion over the region. Their Indian allies humored them by referring to the French king diplomatically as their "father," but to the Indians that term did not imply subservience. In their culture, after all, fathers did not dominate their children—in many ways, it was the father who was obligated and the child who was privileged. Consequently, the Indians felt free to criticize their French patrons and reconsider the relationship.

In 1689, when the Iroquois rallied and attacked French settlements along the Saint Lawrence River, Ottawas began to wonder aloud if it would be best to appease the Iroquois and their English allies. In response, the French colonial governor sent troops to reassure the waverers and issued a proclamation likening the nations of the Iroquois to "five muskrat lodges in a marsh which the French propose to drain and burn." That commitment on the part of the governor evidently satisfied one prominent Ottawa chief, who advised his people: "Vomit forth thy hateful feelings and all thy plots. Return to thy Father, who stretches out his arms and who is, moreover, not unable to protect thee."

In years to come, French and Indian assaults left many Iroquois lodges in flames. At last, in 1701, the Iroquois made peace with the French and their partners in the western lakes region. Even in the tranquil period that ensued, however, the fur trade remained a grueling and uncertain business. Traders taking the main route west from Montreal and Quebec left the Saint Lawrence beyond Montreal, traveled up the Ottawa River,

Men use a towline to "track" a canoe up the rapids, as voyageurs haul their cargo upriver. The grueling work of paddling, portaging, and tracking canoes required a special breed of men. "They are short, thickset, and active, and never tire," said U.S. Indian agent Thomas McKenney in 1826.

portaged to Lake Nipissing, and followed the French River to Georgian Bay and Lake Huron. Others continued up the Saint Lawrence and on through Lakes Ontario and Erie before heading up past Fort Pontchartrain, at the budding village of Detroit, and proceeding to Lake Huron.

Both routes were arduous. In 1684, while the Iroquois wars were still raging, Baron de Lahontan described the struggle of his military party to mount the rapids just above Montreal. His men "were forced to stand in the water up to their middles in order to drag the canoes against the stream," he related. Soon after, they reached a falls and had to carry their canoes and provisions for a half-mile, then portage again for a quarter-mile at another falls some distance farther along. After paddling across a lake, they portaged for a mile and a half around yet another stretch of white water. At every stroke and step of the way, they were assaulted by mosquitoes and black flies. In desperation, the men tried to smoke the pests away, noted Lahontan, but "the remedy was worse than the disease." He and his men might have been better off smearing themselves with bear grease, as some Indians of the region did to keep bugs from biting. French traders who traveled regularly among native peoples adopted many such customs of the country.

No matter how long or difficult their journey, the French made certain to indulge the Indians' love of ceremony. When a chief who was displaying a French flag approached a fortified trading post, booming cannon rendered the salute. Appropriate medals, flags, and other marks of honor were bestowed, and earnest speeches of everlasting peace, amity, and security delivered. Highlighting the welcoming ceremonies were the presents—guns and ammunition, tobacco, kegs of the rum Indians had come to cherish, metal tools, blankets, clothing, and beads.

One French trader among the Ojibwa at Chequamegon gave groups of goods separately to men, women, and children and charmed the recipients by attaching a symbolic value to each item. To the men he presented a kettle, two hatchets, six knives, and a sword blade—the kettle to signify feasting and friendship, the hatchets to strengthen young men against their enemies, and the knives and sword blade to show that France was both mighty and dependable, able to shield its friends and annihilate its foes. In return for such gifts, the trader could expect ample rewards in the form of pelts, but the ritual of exchange was designed to afford each side the honor of appearing trustworthy and magnanimous. Sometimes the Frenchmen dealt with native intermediaries they called trading captains, who represented kinship groups or clans. Most of what the trading captains received they then distributed to those who depended on them, which enabled the captain to enhance his reputation for fairness and generosity. Traders who understood and accommodated tribal values in such ways found the Indians more than willing to ply them with the beaver skins for which the white men had such a hankering.

Obtaining those skins was no difficult task for a people who were familiar with every bend in the stream. The beaver were conspicuous, gnawing down saplings and small trees to construct large lodges and dams in ponds and waterways throughout the area. Hunting took place in winter, when beaver pelts were at their thickest. In addition to shooting and trapping the animals, the Indians broke into the lodges and drove out the beaver. Frequently, the creatures hid in underground passageways leading from their lodges and had to be extracted by hand, which sometimes cost the hunter wounds inflicted by the beaver's sizable teeth. Stretched and dried, the pelts were made up into packs of 40 or 50 skins each to await the spring trading season.

French authorities attempted to regulate the fur trade by selling licenses. Some who purchased them were traders who made the journeys themselves, but others were merchants, who hired men known as voyageurs to carry out the expeditions. Officially, reported Baron de Lahontan in 1685, only 25 licenses were issued each year at a cost of 600 crowns apiece, but hundreds of unofficial traders skirted the law and dealt with the Indians without a license. They did so upon "pain of death," noted Lahontan, for they were cheating the Crown of revenue, but the stricture was exceedingly difficult to enforce.

Those traders who purchased licenses were entitled to fill two canoes, which held trade goods worth about 1,000 crowns—and would fetch 160 packs of beaver skins worth about 8,000 crowns (the traders, Lahontan explained, knew how to "bite the savages most dexterously"). From this sum, the merchant would deduct the cost of his license and goods and pay his voyageurs, who usually ventured out three to a canoe. They received "little more than 600 crowns apiece," Lahontan added, and it was fairly earned, "for their fatigue is inconceivable." Consequently, merchants came away with a tidy profit of 2,500 crowns or so.

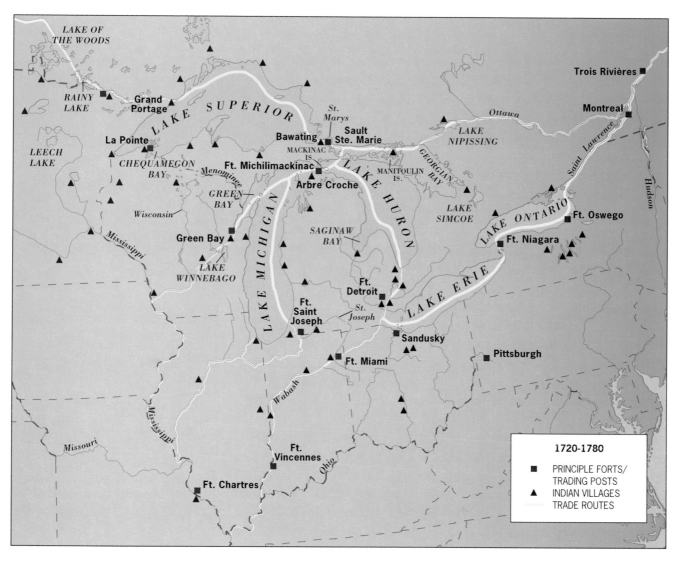

Indian, European, and métis fur traders traveled these major routes during the 18th century, transporting pelts and the trade goods whites offered for them between Indian villages and European trading posts.

Voyageurs seldom lingered long between expeditions to the Great Lakes. Those who had wives in Montreal or Quebec might return home for a while, Lahontan observed, but the bachelors were as careless with their earnings as most sailors of the day: "They lavish, eat, drink, and play all away as long as the goods hold out." When their pay was exhausted, many of them fell to selling the fancy clothes they had just purchased: "This done, they are forced to go upon a new voyage for subsistence." Their journeys often lasted a year or more, and they became familiar presences among the people of the lakes. The Indians grew to admire the tough, unruly, largely uneducated men of the woods. As Ojibwa chronicler William Warren later put it, native peoples saw much of themselves in these voyageurs, with their "continual effervescence of animal spirits, openheartedness, and joviality." The admiration was mutual, and voyageurs took to tribal ways so freely that Indian agent Nicolas Perrot remarked that they had made themselves "like unto the Indians." Many of them took Indian wives, thereby cementing the bonds and fostering a class of mixed-blood métis, who would play a large role in the fur trade and in subsequent French Canadian history.

Such a man was Joseph La France, born about 1707 at Michilimackinac. The son of a French trader and an Ojibwa mother, La France entered the world at a time of crisis for the beaver trade. Fearful of British inroads, the French had kept trading aggressively, until by the late 1690s, the warehouses were filled to overflowing. At that point, the government suddenly abandoned its trading system. Licenses were revoked, and the western trading posts were shut down. The hiatus ended in 1715, after Paris felt makers working through the stocks discovered that much of the hoard had been so poorly stored it was worthless. Soon, the posts at Michilimackinac and other important centers were reopened; prices climbed, and the fur trade rebounded. In the meantime, however, tribes had suffered a loss of trade goods upon which they increasingly depended, and many voyageurs had been denied a livelihood—unless, of course, they found ways to trade with the British at Albany or at Fort Oswego on the eastern shore of Lake Ontario.

Joseph La France's father survived the crisis and even managed to take his boy to Quebec for instruction in French. Returning home, young Joseph learned the rudiments of trade before his father died when he was 14, and at 16, he entered business on his own without a license. For the next decade, he hunted and traded among his mother's people on the northeast shore of Lake Superior. But when the commandant at Michilimackinac granted another trader a license there, La France was forced to seek opportunity elsewhere.

In the spring of 1736, he enlisted the help of eight Iroquois—who were skilled in traveling undetected through the region—and took two canoes loaded with pelts down Lake Huron to the Saint Clair River. That route took him past the French fort of Pontchartrain, which was there not only to keep the British from reaching the upper Great Lakes but also to keep opportunistic traders such as La France from reaching the British. His party took care to slip past the fort under cover of darkness and continued along Lake Erie to Niagara Falls, where they avoided another French stronghold at the mouth of the Niagara River. Portaging around the falls, they at last reached Fort Oswego, where the Iroquois handled the trading arrangements with the British while La France hid in the woods.

Voyageurs set up camp on the shore of a lake at the end of a day of trading with Indian hunters. The voyageurs, acting as middlemen, bought furs from the Indians and sold them to export companies.

The trip proved profitable enough, but the dangers and difficulties helped persuade La France to abandon his illegal ways and seek a French license. Traveling to Montreal the next year, he offered the governor general payment of 1,000 crowns and a pack of marten skins as a gift. The governor general accepted both the money and the pelts, but denied La France a license—and for good measure, charged him with illegally selling brandy to the Indians. La France avoided detention by hastily returning home, only to cross paths the following year with the governor general's brother-in-law as he was traveling down the French River on a supply mission to Michilimackinac. He arrested La France as a fugitive and seized all his goods but failed to keep a close watch on the cagey métis, who escaped in the night with musket and ammunition. La France spent six weeks working his way through the rugged country north of Georgian Bay until he met with Ojibwas from the Mississauga village, who helped him reach Sault Sainte Marie.

It was not only métis such as La France who had problems with

An 18th-century engraving captures the meeting of two cultures as Europeans receive in trade a pelt prized for use in hats and clothing. Equally precious to Indians were the goods obtained in exchange, examples of which appear on the following pages.

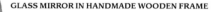

GLASS MIRROR IN HANDMADE WOODEN FRAME

COPPER TEAKETTLE

French officials. In the early 18th century, the French had come up with a plan to deal with tribal bands that had remained around Green Bay and were disrupting French trade with the rival Dakota Sioux to their west. The French invited the Green Bay groups—including the Fox—to resettle near Fort Pontchartrain. The plan went awry when those Fox who agreed to resettle began to feud with Indians who were already residing at the fort and their French protectors. The dispute escalated until the Fox at Fort Pontchartrain were attacked and crushed by the French and their Indian allies. Some members of the Fox tribe escaped and stirred up further resistance to French traders among their relatives who had remained behind at Green Bay. The French responded with a series of attacks that finally subdued the tribe. Many of the Fox were killed or captured, while those who remained free ultimately sought protection among the Sauk.

As this bitter episode made clear, the French were finding it increasingly difficult to reconcile the conflicting demands of their various native trading partners. The Ojibwas living around the western end of Lake Su-

**LARGE BRASS KETTLE PATCHED WITH
METAL SCRAPS AND HOMEMADE RIVETS**

FLINTLOCK MUSKET WITH SERPENT SIDEPLATE

perior, for their part, bristled at French efforts to trade directly with their traditional foes, the Dakota Sioux. In recent times, the Ojibwa had kept the peace and served as middlemen between Dakota hunters and French traders. But as the French disposed of Fox opposition and extended their reach westward to the Mississippi River and beyond, they no longer needed the Ojibwa as intermediaries in order to obtain pelts from the Dakota, whose territory abounded with beaver. The Ojibwa responded by pushing into Dakota hunting grounds to regain their advantage in the trade. Inevitably, such intrusions spurred retaliation, and the old adversaries went at each other with a vengeance.

This new phase of the Dakota-Ojibwa conflict began in the 1730s and continued thereafter for many decades, seesawing back and forth in countless deadly ambushes and raids. William Warren, drawing on accounts handed down by Ojibwa warriors, told of one such contest that took place in the 1760s at the confluence of the Crow Wing and Mississippi Rivers, just west of Mille Lacs. Having allied themselves with the Assiniboin and the Cree to the northwest—both of them longtime foes of the Sioux—the Ojibwa had slowly gained the upper hand and forced the Dakota to evacuate their villages at Mille Lacs and retreat south to the Rum River. "Smarting under the loss of their ancient village sites, and their best

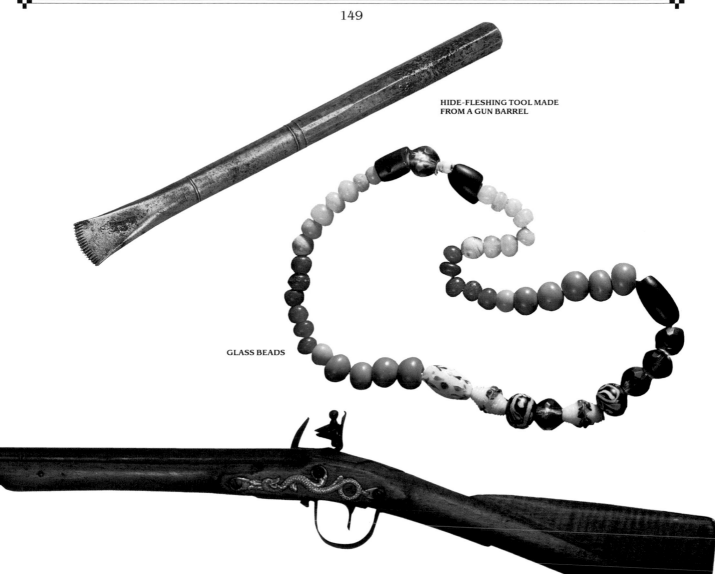

HIDE-FLESHING TOOL MADE
FROM A GUN BARREL

GLASS BEADS

hunting grounds and rice lakes," related Warren, "the Sioux determined to make one more united and national effort to stem the advance of their troublesome and persevering enemies, and drive them back to the shores of Lake Superior."

A war party of more than 400 Dakotas proceeded up the Mississippi to its headwaters, planning to assault the Ojibwa village at Sandy Lake. Along the way, they killed and scalped a number of Ojibwa hunters and took captive 30 young women gathering berries near Sandy Lake. The village itself appeared to be easy pickings. Sixty of the best Ojibwa warriors had just departed on a raid of their own, and as the attackers approached the settlement, they could hear from the shouts and general din that the place was in panic. Many of the remaining warriors were drunk on firewater obtained from traders, and the women were frantically trying to sober them up by ducking their heads in cold water.

The Dakotas attacked forthwith. It was a close fight, but the women managed to brace enough of their menfolk to withstand the assault. At length, the Dakotas retreated with their handful of scalps and the 30 captive women. The warriors, recounted Warren, "were doomed, however, to run a severe gantlet before reaching their villages."

To the south, the Ojibwa raiding party, having found no enemies, was returning home when it came upon a campsite recently abandoned by Dakotas. From the tracks, the warriors guessed where their enemies had been heading—to assault their families at Sandy Lake. With cold fury, they laid an ambush just below the confluence of the Crow Wing and the Mississippi Rivers. Here stood a high bluff against which the powerful river current would draw the enemy canoes. The Ojibwa warriors dug ditches in the earthen bluff for concealment—and waited.

In due course, continued Warren, an Ojibwa scout "saw the whole bosom of the river covered with war canoes." The Sioux disembarked in view of the concealed Ojibwas and roughly forced the captive women—among them relatives of the anxious warriors—to cook their morning meal. After eating, they set out once more in a compact mass, accompanied by much chanting. At last the moment had come for the waiting Ojibwas: "At the sound of their leader's war whistle, they suddenly let fly a flight of bullets and barbed arrows into the serried ranks of their enemies, picking out for death the most prominent and full plumed figures amongst them."

All was chaos among the Sioux. At the first volley, the captive women overturned the canoes in which they were riding and struck out for shore. Other canoes capsized from the convulsions of wounded men. Many Sioux drowned, and others were picked off as they swam for safety. The survivors struggled ashore and collected themselves below the ambush site. They sensed that comparatively few Ojibwas were involved and, burning for revenge, they counterattacked. The fighting lasted until nightfall, with the entrenched Ojibwas suffering no losses and the Sioux taking further punishment. The Sioux tried to overcome their attackers again the following morning, and by that time, Ojibwa ammunition was running low. The opponents fought hand to hand with stones and knives and war clubs. Yet in the end, the Ojibwas emerged victorious. The badly mauled Sioux "returned to

Decorated with war paint and grasping a bow and arrow, a Fox warrior epitomizes the courageous fighting spirit for which the tribe was known.

their villages," concluded Warren, "and for fear that the Ojibwas would retaliate, by making a similar incursion, evacuated the Rum River country and moved to the Minnesota River."

The fur trade not only gave impetus to such tribal wars but also embroiled the native peoples of the region in the epic conflict between France and Britain that simmered for decades and came to a boil in the 1750s. By then, the British colonists in the New World far outnumbered the French, who had never succeeded in luring great numbers of settlers from the motherland to brave the fierce winters and forbidding back country. To the south, by contrast, there were so many English speakers living along the Atlantic seaboard that streams of land-hungry pioneers were spilling over the Allegheny Mountains into western New York, Pennsylvania, and Ohio. Anxious to protect their fur empire, the French armed the tribes of the upper Great Lakes and sent warriors under French officers to terrorize British frontier settlements, all the while claiming that they had no control over their "savages." The Indians went at their task with a will. Some of them had quarreled with the French at times, but they were bound to them by trading ties, reinforced in many cases by family connections—and they too were eager to stem the westward flow of British colonists.

The skirmishing erupted into outright warfare along the frontier in 1754. Known to the British as the French and Indian War, the conflict in North America was linked to the wider Seven Years' War that began in Europe in 1756 and dragged on until 1763. Great Lakes Indians from such places as Sault Sainte Marie, Michilimackinac, Green Bay, and Detroit fought alongside the French in battle after battle against the British—who profited by some Indian support of their own from groups such as the Mohawk, the easternmost nation of the Iroquois.

This fearsome Ojibwa war club was crafted of materials obtained in trade: a wooden gunstock wedded to a spike of iron. The weapon bears artistically incised figures, which often denoted a warrior's guardian spirit.

For a time, the French and their Indian allies prevailed in the conflict. In 1755 a French contingent of about 300 soldiers and a mixed Indian force of nearly 1,000 warriors overwhelmed 1,500 British troops on their way to retake Fort

Located at the juncture of Lakes Superior, Huron, and Michigan, Mackinac Island became the hub of the Great Lakes fur trade. In the sketch, the British fortress overlooks a harbor where ships lie ready to exchange goods for beaver pelts and other furs.

Two Ottawa chiefs from Michilimackinac display their bartered assets—silver ornaments and trade-cloth garments—in a watercolor by a British artist in the early 1800s.

SIR JOS JEBB.

Duquesne at present-day Pittsburgh, fatally wounding their commander, General Edward Braddock, and inflicting nearly 1,000 casualties on his dazed followers. Credit for the stunning victory belonged in large part to warriors from the lakes region, led by a mixed-blood Ottawa named Charles Langlade from Michilimackinac.

In 1756 a joint force including nearly 1,000 Indians—among them Ojibwas, Ottawas, and Potawatomis—captured Fort Oswego on Lake Ontario. In 1757 Charles Langlade again took the lead in a successful attack, capturing Fort William Henry on Lake Champlain. But the campaign turned against the French and their Indian allies at Fort Duquesne in the fall of 1758. At first, they defended the place skillfully against a British advance guard. But then the warriors returned to their villages to prepare for the winter months, and the remaining French were unable to hold off the main British force. By 1760 both Quebec and Montreal had fallen to the British—despite the best efforts of warriors from the lakes region—and British troops pushed on to Detroit.

Canada soon belonged to Great Britain. But the people of the lakes—many of whom now spoke French in addition to their native tongues—retained that element of their heritage. (Even today, many Indians of the region go by French surnames and hail one another with a brisk *boo-zhoo:* "bonjour.") Nor did the warriors who battled the British feel in the least defeated. Indians returned home brimming with good spirits in canoes loaded with booty. The king of France, they would say, had simply gone to sleep and would "shortly awaken to return to his children." One Ojibwa chief told a British trader: "Englishman, although you have conquered the French, you have not conquered us. We are not your slaves!"

It angered prominent Indians such as the Ottawa chief Pontiac to hear from a British Indian agent that they would "enjoy free trade and possession of the country as long as they adhered to His Majesty's wishes." The ill will was compounded by the British military governor, Lord Jeffrey Amherst, who disdained Indians as a race and had once suggested to a subordinate that blankets infected with smallpox be spread among the native allies of the French. Amherst tried to discourage traders from giving presents to influential Indians—a practice that he denounced as mere "bribery" but the Indians considered common courtesy.

Furthermore, the British restricted the flow of weapons to the region, which made it harder for hunters to provide for their families. The British had no such scruples, however, when it came to trading liquor, a commodity that the French too had dealt in but that was now offered so widely to Indians that it became known as "English milk." One Lake Superior trader described a drunken "frolic" that lasted four days and sparked fighting that left three Indians dead and six wounded. This trader, like others, found that he could still sell the Indians plenty of rum, but quiet "their impertinence" by lacing it with opium.

All of this might have been bearable had it not been clear to Pontiac and other discerning chieftains that the British intended to occupy and settle their land. Unlike the French, they would not be content with a few forts and trading posts around the lakes. They would have to be driven out. The planning for Pontiac's War, as it became known, went on for an entire year. When the allied Indians struck in the spring of 1763, the British were caught almost entirely by surprise. Between May 8 and June 22, well-coordinated parties of Ottawas, Ojibwas, and warriors from other tribes attacked every British fort west of the Alleghenies. There were 11 in all, including some acquired from the French. By late summer, only the bastions at Detroit and Pittsburgh remained in British hands—and both of those were under siege. The other nine had been taken by the Indians, who had slaughtered most of their garrisons.

The attackers had relied on subterfuge to penetrate the fortifications. The June 4 attack on Fort Michilimackinac was a classic of its kind. Approximately 90 British regulars commanded by a major defended the fort. To deal with them, the renowned Ojibwa war chief Matchekewis mustered several hundred Ojibwas and visiting Sauks. By no coincidence, June 4 was the birthday of the British king George III, and Matchekewis informed the commandant that his young men would honor the occasion with a match of lacrosse—a game that was played between two goals but knew no bounds, since the contestants would chase after the ball with their sticks wherever it went. No obstacle was allowed to stand in the way of getting at the ball, explained William Warren: "Were it to fall into the chimney of a house, a jump through the window or a smash of the door would be considered of no moment."

At the appointed hour, the vying teams of Ojibwas and Sauks appeared, decked out ceremonially in feathers, ribbons, and fox and wolf tails, and hurled themselves after the ball, yelling and whacking at each other with abandon. The fort's commandant stood outside the open gate looking on with rapt attention, while his unarmed soldiers lounged about the fort and mingled with the Indian women sitting nearby. Suddenly, out of the melee, the ball sailed high into the air—and landed inside the fort. "With one deafening yell and impulse," related Warren, "the players rushed

General Edward Braddock falls mortally wounded as warriors of the lakes region fend off British troops on July 9, 1755, near present-day Pittsburgh. Charles Langlade, an officer of French and Ottawa extraction, is pictured at left leading the attack.

forward in a body as if to regain the ball." But as they passed their women, they threw down the lacrosse sticks and snatched up the shortened guns, knives, tomahawks, and war clubs the women had concealed in their robes. On raced the warriors, sweeping through the open gate.

An English trader named Alexander Henry was in a room at the fort writing letters when he heard the war cries and ran to a window. "I saw a crowd of Indians within the fort, furiously cutting down and scalping every Englishman they found," recounted Henry. "I saw several of my countrymen fall, and more than one struggling between the knees of an Indian, who, holding him in this manner, scalped him while yet living." The bloodbath was over quickly. Perhaps 70 of the 90 soldiers were slain, and the rest, including the hapless major, were taken captive. Most of the civilians in and around the fort were French Canadians, and not one suffered harm; by Henry's account, they looked on with equanimity. Only a few British traders were present; one was slain and the others taken prisoner. Henry himself was marked for death, but survived through the intercession of an Ojibwa named Wawatam, whom he had earlier befriended. Wawatam had declared the two of them to be "brothers," and he now took Henry under his protection.

From the security of Wawatam's lodge, Henry witnessed what might have been his own fate when the bodies of seven white men were dragged out onto the parade ground the next morning. The corpse of one victim was then dismembered, and pieces dumped into five kettles, to be boiled into a sort of broth. Invited to participate, Wawatam returned with a bowl in which rested a hand and a piece of flesh. Henry noted that Wawatam "did not appear to relish the repast," but it was still a solemn custom among his people "to make a war feast from among the slain. This, he said, inspired the warrior with courage in attack, and bred him to meet death with fearlessness." Henry spent the next winter hunting in the woods of Michigan with Wawatam and his relatives as their adopted kinsman before he left them and returned to his life as a trader.

Pontiac's War so disturbed the British that they convened a great peace council at Niagara the next summer. The Indians were suspicious at first. The Ojibwas at Sault Sainte Marie consulted an esteemed medicine man, who performed a shaking-tent ceremony and summoned the spirit of the Great Turtle. That manitou assured Ojibwas that if they attended the council, the British would fill their canoes with presents: "blankets, kettles, guns, gunpowder and shot, and large barrels of rum, such as the stoutest of the Indians will not be able to lift; and every man will return in safety to

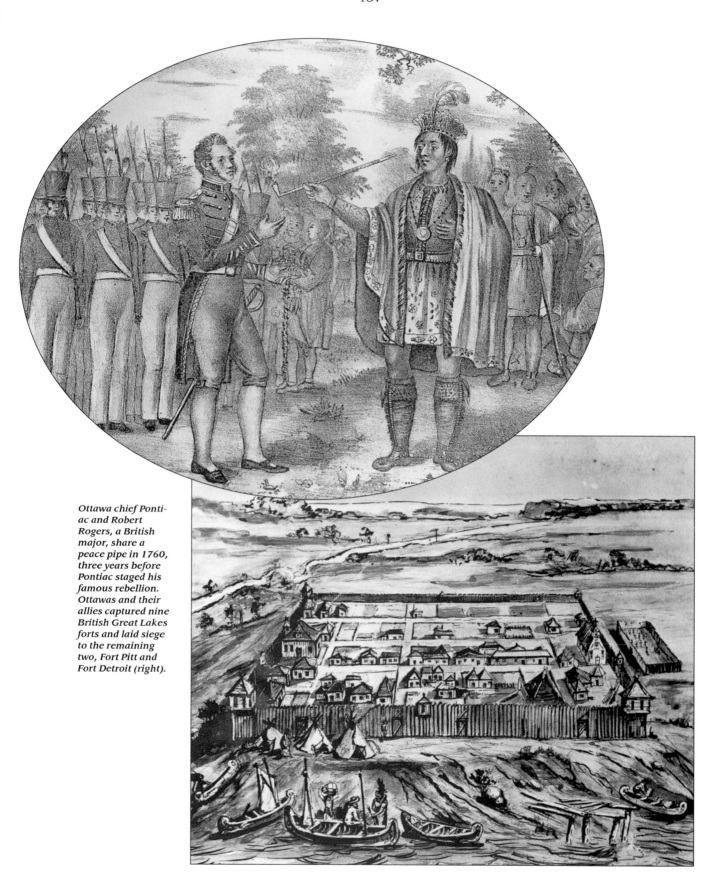

Ottawa chief Pontiac and Robert Rogers, a British major, share a peace pipe in 1760, three years before Pontiac staged his famous rebellion. Ottawas and their allies captured nine British Great Lakes forts and laid siege to the remaining two, Fort Pitt and Fort Detroit (right).

his family." And so it happened. The British not only plied the Indians with gifts but also acknowledged their claims to lands situated beyond the crest of the Alleghenies, including the lakes region. Whites could venture there only to trade, the British decreed. The boundary line was shifted in 1768 by the Treaty of Fort Stanwix, which set the Ohio River as the frontier between Indians and whites, with the land north and west of that river reserved for the original inhabitants.

The agreement proved acceptable to Indians of the lakes region. For tribes whose homelands lay safely beyond the frontier, the treaty and the gifts that accompanied it were signs that the British could be trusted. Indeed, trade blossomed between the Indians and the British after the stormy interlude of Pontiac's War. Among those prominently involved was the former captive Alexander Henry, who in 1765 obtained a license granting him exclusive rights to the trade around Lake Superior from the British commandant at Fort Michilimackinac. For a partner, Henry took a French Canadian métis named Cadotte, who had married an Ojibwa woman and was greatly respected by the Indians. Their trading technique was to advance goods to Indians around the lake for beaver pelts that would be provided after the winter's hunting. A blanket was worth between eight and 10 skins, for example, and a gun, 20 skins. In one season, the partners advanced goods worth 3,000 beaver skins and wound up with 100 families hunting for them. Thanks to such energetic trading and new hunting techniques—including the use of steel traps—more than 50,000 beaver pelts passed through Michilimackinac in 1767 alone.

Such harvests could not long continue without depleting the beaver population in the area. In the meantime, however, the Indians of the Great Lakes faced a more pressing challenge—conflict with that vast group of English speakers who were coming to identify themselves not as British subjects but as Americans. Antagonized in part by the British agreement to bar settlement northwest of the Ohio River, the colonists rose up against the king in 1776 and fought for their independence. The victory of the American colonists in 1783 had devastating repercussions for the region's tribes. In the years that followed, the Americans used questionable land deals and military force to claim much of Ohio. Alarmed by the advances of the whites they called Chemokmon, or Big Knives, for the sabers American militiamen wielded, the people of the lakes looked for support to the British, who still held forts in the region and supplied the Indians with arms. When the British and Americans again came to blows during the War of 1812, the tribes around the lakes sided largely with the British.

Indeed, warriors there began battling Americans long before the United States declared war on Great Britain.

Native opposition to the Americans was organized by the Shawnee chief Tecumseh and his brother, known as the Prophet, whose tribe had lost most of its ancestral territory in Ohio to the Americans and who persuaded tribes to the north and west that they would soon suffer the same fate if they did not oppose the Big Knives. Among those who joined in the fight were Ojibwas, Ottawas, Potawatomis, Winnebagos, Menominees, Sauks, and Foxes. Early on, warriors battling the Big Knives succeeded in overwhelming several outposts acquired by Americans after the Revolution, including the forts at Detroit, Mackinac (the former Michilimackinac), and Chicago, where some 600 Potawatomis massacred scores of soldiers and a small number of civilians after they abandoned Fort Dearborn. These assaults only provoked the Americans, who launched devastating expeditions against Indian villages in Michigan, Indiana, and Illinois. In 1814 the embattled Indians found themselves without white allies when the British—whose forces in the lakes region had been pushed back into Canada and defeated—came to terms with the United States. The tribes still at war with the Big Knives had little choice but to conclude treaties with the United States that were often punitive in nature.

Things would never be the same for the people of the lakes. Lingering American hostility toward the tribes of the region ensured that federal authorities would pressure them remorselessly to yield territory. With the end of the war, settlers surged across the Ohio, many of them farmers attracted by the rich soil at the southern end of the lakes. Where the prospects for farming were dim, mining outfits moved in to extract copper, iron, and lead. By 1820 steamboats were navigating the Great Lakes, which made it easier to get the ore out—and bring the people in. By 1825 the Erie Canal had been completed, swinging wide the gates for emigrants from the east. By 1830 there were 1,700,000 whites in the region, compared with a scant 72,000 Indians.

Many tribal bands in the region had already been threatened or cajoled into surrendering a great deal of their land. In 1819, for example, the territorial governor of Michigan, Lewis Cass, traveled to Saginaw to talk Ojibwa leaders into ceding land. For persuasive effect, Cass brought along a company of U.S. Army troops and a shipment of "presents" that included nearly 200 gallons of liquor. When the assembled Ojibwas refused to

come to terms, traders and interpreters at the council offered individual chiefs inducements of goods, guns, and alcohol to bring them around. When all was said and done, the Ojibwas had signed away roughly six million acres of land in Michigan in exchange for tribal reserves covering little more than 100,000 acres.

Federal negotiators made such land deals more attractive to the Indians by offering them cash annuities. These yearly disbursements of money were sorely needed, for overhunting left the Ojibwa and their neighbors with a dwindling supply of pelts to offer in exchange for the trade goods they had come to rely on. Few of the Indians still made their own tools and clothing. Although they continued to hunt, fish, and gather wild rice, they often needed provisions from traders to get by in lean seasons. For some Indians, however, the annuities seemed poor compensation for what had been taken from them. One Ojibwa chief named Yellow Beaver, who had refused to sign the Saginaw Treaty, appeared there every year to claim his annuity—only to toss the coins he received disdainfully into the river.

In 1837 Potawatomi leaders meet a United States government delegation to conduct negotiations that ultimately resulted in the tribe's removal from its Michigan and Indiana homeland to reservations west of the Mississippi River. The chief Keewaunay is depicted standing at left.

Some tribes in the region were divested of their homelands altogether as part of a federal effort to remove native peoples to the supposedly empty plains west of the Mississippi (a policy that ignored the claims of the many tribes already living there). Among those subjected to removal were the Winnebago, who had rebounded from their setbacks of earlier times and spread out across much of southern Wisconsin. In the 1820s, however, Winnebago territory was overrun by miners prospecting for lead. The miners waged a campaign of harassment so troublesome to the Winnebago that in 1827 they delegated a warrior named Red Bird to exact revenge. With some reluctance, Red Bird and two cohorts attacked a white homestead near Prairie du Chien, killing several people, after which Red Bird surrendered to forestall a vigilante-style reprisal. The United States government used the incident to impose a treaty in 1829 that stripped the tribe of half of its territory south of the Wisconsin River. Mixed-bloods and Indian wives of white men were allowed to remain in the ceded area, but all other Winnebagos had to depart. Another treaty three years later further reduced the tribe's domain.

The government acknowledged that the tribe's remaining land in Wisconsin could not support all those who were displaced and subsequently granted the Winnebago a reservation on the Turkey River in Iowa. But that place was a no man's land, hotly contested between bands of Dakota Sioux and the Sauk, who had been forced there from Illinois despite fierce resistance from their war chief Black Hawk. The newcomers soon found themselves embroiled in hostilities. Alarmed by the experience, the Winnebago refused a fresh demand by the government that those still in Wisconsin cede their remaining territory and move west. Under pressure, however, they did agree to send a delegation to Washington in 1837. Tribal leaders purposely limited the power of the delegation by appointing men of little or no authority; among those absent were leaders of the Bear Clan, which policed the tribe. Nonetheless, officials in Washington pressured the delegates into making a major commitment for the tribe by holding them as virtual prisoners until they signed away the remaining land. Upon returning home, the Winnebagos discovered that they had been not only coerced but deceived. They had been told that they would have eight years to vacate the land; the treaty they signed in fact allowed for only eight months. An interpreter later confessed that he had been ordered to mislead the delegates.

This fraud permanently split the Winnebago peoples. The majority of them accepted removal but pressed for a viable reservation of their own.

In 1855 they at last received one—at Blue Earth in southern Minnesota. There they took up farming with a will, donned what was called "citizen's dress," curbed the use of liquor, and built a jail to confine wrongdoers. Men from the community even enlisted to fight for the Union in the Civil War. But none of that prevented them from losing their reservation when an uprising by the Dakota Sioux in Minnesota prompted authorities to remove not only the Dakotas but also the peaceful Winnebagos, who were sent to a desolate tract on Crow Creek in South Dakota. By the end of the first brutal winter there, 552 of the 1,934 Winnebagos taken from Blue Earth had died of cold, starvation, or disease. The survivors, almost to a person, ignored the threats of their guards and escaped south in dugout canoes to find shelter among Omahas who were living along the Missouri River in Nebraska. There, in 1865, they signed a final treaty giving up the hated Crow Creek to start life anew on land carved from the northern edge of the Omaha reservation.

The other faction of perhaps 1,000 or so Winnebagos refused to leave Wisconsin after the treaty of 1837 and camped in the woods of central Wisconsin as fugitives. From time to time, government agents rounded up as many as they could find and transported them to the current Winnebago reservation, but most of them found their way back to Wisconsin within a year or two. Finally, in 1881, they were allowed to apply for 40-acre homesteads there. The land they acquired was among the poorest in the state and was capable of supporting only small gardens, which they supplemented through traditional subsistence activities. But no longer did authorities seek to displace them.

Members of other tribes in the region resisted removal to the west as well. When Potawatomis living in southern Michigan and northern Indiana were relocated to a reservation in Kansas in 1841, some members of the tribe who had adapted to European ways stayed behind and formed small communities much like those of the white settlers pouring into the area. Others chose to migrate to the Canadian province of Ontario, where members of various tribal groups intermingled on Walpole Island, east of Detroit, as well as in more remote areas. Both Ottawas and Ojibwas, for example, found refuge in large numbers on Manitoulin Island—or Spirit Island—and intermarried to such an extent that the native population there today is best described simply as Anishinabe. So strong was the attachment to tradition that many western reservation dwellers returned to the lakes region eventually and found homes on and off reservations.

Some groups, such as the Menominee of northern Wisconsin and the

Winnebago chief Winneshiek (center) and his followers are shown during their confinement at Fort Snelling in Minnesota in 1863. The chief was arrested for his continued resistance to his tribe's removal to a reservation.

Ojibwas living around Lake Superior, never left their homelands, but they found it difficult to retain the territory set aside for them by treaty. By the mid-1800s, federal interest in removing the Indians to the west was waning, in part because the Plains were proving more attractive to white settlers than the tracts of forest and marsh reserved for the people of the lakes. Yet the ruggedness of the land did not keep outsiders from maneuvering to take what they could. Time and again, federal authorities satisfied mining outfits or timber companies by pressing tribal leaders to cede more territory in exchange for annuities that did little to ease the poverty of reservation dwellers.

Although treaties typically entitled Indians to hunt and fish on the

land they ceded, native peoples who did so often met with hostility. Whites in Minnesota objected menacingly in 1864 when some Ojibwas left their reservations to hunt deer. The "game belonged to white folks," insisted the *St. Paul Daily Press,* which advised all Indian "whelps" to remain behind reservation boundaries or "else some of them may accidentally be taken for deer by our hunters." It was no idle threat, for whites who killed Indians were seldom punished—and sometimes rewarded. The year before, Minnesota authorities had responded to an abortive uprising by a handful of starving Ojibwas by placing a bounty on Indian scalps. Proclaimed the *St. Paul Pioneer Press:* "Good News For Indian Hunters—The Indian-hunting trade is likely to prove a profitable investment to our hunters and scouts in the Big Woods, the Commander-in-Chief having increased the bounty for each top-knot of a 'bloody heathen' to $200."

Missionaries on the reservations tried to show Indians that whites

The treaty-abiding Winnebagos, shown here in a council with Omaha Indians, were pushed west in a series of land cessions, finally sharing a Nebraska reservation with the Omaha in 1865.

A grim-looking Winnebago delegation to Washington in 1912 displays old treaties, testifying to the history of travails the tribe endured at the hands of the United States government.

could be trusted and had much to offer them spiritually and culturally. Yet like the Jesuits of the French era, these mission workers found it difficult to win over people who were so deeply attached to the beliefs of their ancestors. In 1869 President Ulysses S. Grant placed the nation's reservations under the control of missionary boards, and many Indians went along with the new regime by accepting baptism or sending their children to missionary schools. But among the people of the lakes, the obeisance was often superficial. The children in mission schools recited their lessons dutifully, but many cut class whenever they could. Christian ministers remained outsiders, and church attendance proved disappointing; in private and in times of crisis, the Indians turned to their ancestral practices. Some tribal leaders remarked that if God had meant the Indians to have the white man's religion, he would have given them the Bible in their own language. Indeed, members of the Midewiwin, or Grand Medicine Society—who opposed the efforts to convert Indians—insisted that the Great Spirit had already spoken to the Anishinabe through the sacred scrolls.

Attachment to native traditions surfaced in a different form in the late 19th century when a movement known as the Dream Dance spread among the people of the lakes. Originating among the Dakota Sioux about 1877, the movement's central legend explained how a young girl had escaped the slaughter of her band by army soldiers by hiding in the shallows of a lake for many days. Then, just as she was about to collapse from hunger, a force lifted her from the water and a voice spoke to her: "Be not afraid," it said, "you have been chosen to receive a message from heaven." The voice promised that the Great Spirit would protect all Indians from the white man, and it instructed her in a new "dream dance," involving a distinctive blue, red, and yellow drum and other regalia that would put her people in touch with the Supreme Being. For a while, the movement served as a rallying force for some Indians of the Great Lakes. Dancers called for the revival of ancient traditions and preached a spirit of friend-

A many-sided Ojibwa lodge photographed in 1910 served as a gathering place for participants in the Dream Dance, the religious movement that promised a new dawn of freedom for the Indians.

ship among the tribes. The enthusiasm eventually diminished, as Indians lost hope that any force could defend them against the ever-multiplying whites. Yet many native peoples of the region remained convinced that spirit power came to them through sacred dances and other traditional observances.

As the 19th century drew to a close, one defiant band of Ojibwas briefly found itself at war with the United States. The fighting occurred on October 5, 1898,

A sacred Dream Dance drum is offered to Menominee participants at an intertribal ceremony in Wisconsin in 1928. Such drums (left), decorated with paint and beadwork, sit supported by four feathered stakes representing the cardinal directions: north, south, east, and west.

With women driving the wagons, Kickapoo migrants struggle across a rough tableland near the Texas border about 1904. They soon joined other tribe members who had settled on land provided by the Mexican government near the town of Nacimiento in the mid-19th century.

ONE TRIBE'S DISTANT EXILE

A Kickapoo village in northern Mexico consists of traditional domed houses, cooking sheds, and summer arbors, known as ramadas.

No Great Lakes tribe moved farther from its original homeland to escape wars and white encroachment than the Kickapoo, a people related to the Sauk and Fox. Living in the woodlands of what is now western Wisconsin when French explorers first arrived, the Kickapoo soon retreated to the Wabash Valley of Indiana and Illinois before moving westward into Missouri. From there most of the tribe trekked southwest into the plains of Oklahoma, Texas, and even Mexico—where several hundred remain to this day.

Despite their long exiles in alien lands, the Kickapoo have retained a remarkable number of their ancient religious festivals, ways of dress, and other customs. Many still hunt for much of their food and live in rounded dwellings made of poles covered with rush mats, just as their ancestors did in their Great Lakes villages centuries ago.

In a photograph taken about 1927, 15-year-old Standard Wilde, a Kickapoo living in Mexico, is shown wearing a dazzlingly ornate dance costume that he made himself.

at Leech Lake, a small reservation in north-central Minnesota. The incident attracted relatively little notice at a time when newspapers were heralding the victorious conclusion of the Spanish-American War. This remote skirmish offered white Americans nothing to boast about, either in its origins or in its outcome.

About 1,100 Ojibwas inhabited the Leech Lake Reservation, making their livelihood by hunting, fishing, harvesting wild rice, and selling fallen timber from their forests. They were basically peaceful, but increasingly aggrieved. The U.S. Army Corps of Engineers had outraged the Indians in the 1880s by flooding 40,000 acres of prime wild rice swamps. Moreover, since Minnesota law officers received a fee for each arrest, deputy marshals made a regular practice of picking up Ojibwa men, usually on charges of selling liquor illegally or as witnesses to that traffic; as often as not, the arresting officer had helped supply the offending liquor.

One prominent target for such harassment was Bugonegijig, a 62-year-old chief known to whites as Old Bug. The authorities detained him more than once as a witness or suspect in the liquor traffic and made plans to arrest him again when he arrived at the Leech Lake Agency on September 15 to collect his annuity distribution. A deputy marshal slapped him behind bars, but some 50 Ojibwas snatched him away and escorted him home to Sugar Point, on the northeast shore of Leech Lake. Bent on recapturing the fugitive, the United States marshal in Saint Paul called for reinforcements. In due course, a contingent of 100 U.S. Army infantrymen and a handful of Indian police, commanded by a brevet major and accompanied by a brigadier general,

Ojibwa chief Bugonegijig (left) poses with members of his tribe in 1897, a year before he became involved in a struggle against oppressive government authority at Leech Lake Reservation in Minnesota.

arrived by train at the town of Walker on the southwest shore of the lake.

On the snowy morning of October 5, the force chugged up the lake in two small steamers and a barge. When the soldiers stormed ashore at Sugar Point, they found only a few Indians there. The troops, mostly raw recruits, marched about for a while without encountering resistance, then relaxed. They were in the process of stacking arms for the noon lunch break when one of the rifles accidentally discharged. "There was a moment of ominous silence," recalled a soldier. Then the troops discovered that they were not alone. From the enveloping woods, the soldier related, "Indians poured a most terrific volley into our ranks. We found ourselves almost entirely surrounded by the enemy."

Frantically, the troops scrambled for their rifles and took cover, eventually forming a rough skirmish line. But the Indians kept lashing them with fire and pinned them down. From time to time, a concealed Ojibwa would let out a war cry, "chilling the very marrow in our bones," recalled one wounded private. Meanwhile, the steamers, having come under fire, stood off Sugar Point and then returned to Walker. The troops were on their own, to either fight it out or be driven into the lake. But the Ojibwas were content to hold the army at bay. After three and a half hours, the firing eased and the soldiers made camp for the night. The next day, the following telegram from Minnesota reached authorities in Washington: "Commenced fighting at 11:30 yesterday. Indians seem to have best position. Not moving. Maj. Wilkinson, five soldiers and two Indian police killed; awaiting reinforcements."

By the time the telegram arrived, another 214 troops had already been dispatched to the trouble spot with a Gatling gun. Ultimately, the number of troops at Leech Lake swelled to 1,000. The area was cordoned off, but there was no further fighting. Wisely, the commissioner of Indian affairs, William A. Jones, traveled to Leech Lake and invited the Ojibwas to come in for a parley. They were agreeable and accepted a canoeload of presents, including pork, flour, sugar, and tobacco.

No one was sure how many Indians had participated in the combat—perhaps only 20 or so, armed with a motley array of rifles and shotguns. Privately, they took a certain pride in what they had accomplished. In the end, a dozen of the chief's followers received sentences of from 60 days to 10 months—which were later commuted by presidential pardon. As for the chief himself, he never was arrested, but continued to live free. He made himself a bright necklace of spent U.S. Army cartridge shells and delighted his people by telling them how he had invoked his powers as a medicine man and changed himself into a bird when the fighting broke out. As befitted a leader of advanced age, he had watched over his warriors from a lofty perch, relishing their victory.

As this incident underscored, the Ojibwa remained proud and independent. The relative isolation of their reservations helped them withstand the intrusions of white civilization better than most tribes. Many of them continued to pursue a seasonal round that included visits to hunting camps in the winter, sugarbushes in the spring, and wild rice fields in late summer. They preserved their language, much of their religion, and their knowledge of herbal medicines. By the 1920s, however, the virgin forests were disappearing under the saw. The timber business declined, and the Ojibwa lost income that had helped to make up for the moribund fur trade. Many of them descended into the same bitter poverty as that experienced by members of other tribes.

The people of the lakes, who had little to spend in the best of times, suffered dearly during the depression of the 1930s. At the Ojibwa's Fond du Lac Reservation in Minnesota, average family income fell to $310, most of it from menial, part-time jobs. Government schools did little to improve the prospects of native children; the Indian police corps withered for want of candidates willing to accept such a thankless task.

For many native peoples of the region, the only solution was to move off the reservations and seek work elsewhere. During World War II, thousands of Indians left tribal communities to work in factories and shipyards in urban areas or to serve in the armed forces. In the 1950s, the government prompted further relocation by encouraging Indians to leave reservations and migrate to Chicago, Detroit, Minneapolis, and other major cities. By the mid-1970s, almost 12,000 of Minnesota's 22,322 Native Americans were city dwellers.

Some agencies and educators endeavored to keep the traditions alive. In the 1970s, the Indian Education Act gave reservation parents a say in how federal funds are spent in local schools. In recent years, some reservations have established their own community colleges, and the Ojibwas at Lac Court Oreilles in Wisconsin have maintained their own radio station. Profits from legal gambling operations have helped some tribal councils build schools, housing, and community centers. And native groups have asserted their treaty rights to fish, hunt, and harvest on their traditional grounds located off the reservation.

Among the enduring customs of the people of the lakes is the wild rice harvest. Indians around the region have long sold some of the rice

Their lands reduced and their traditions challenged, Ojibwa men on a reservation in Minnesota meet in council in 1900. Lamenting the impact of government policies on the Indians' way of life, a 19th-century Ojibwa leader commented, "The warm wave of the white man rolls upon us and melts us away."

they picked to help support their families. But in recent decades, wild rice has become big business, and some tribal groups have begun to compete for their share of a growing market by cultivating the crop in paddies—a practice that worries traditionalists, who fear that the manomin, or "spirit seed," will lose its ritual significance.

Today, Indians of the lakes region still venture out in canoes onto lakes and marshes to beat the grains from the stalks with sticks. City dwellers make a point of rejoining old friends and relatives for the festive occasion, which for many families still involves offering rice to the spirits in a first-fruit ceremony. "We have a deep feeling of satisfaction and gratitude as we sack up the rice again toward evening," remarked Ojibwa Norma Smith of the Mole Lake Reservation in northern Wisconsin. "We do not feel the ache in our arms as we anticipate the gain. If the rice is light, we will sell it for seed. If it is heavy, we will take it home to cure for eating. And tomorrow we will be back for another day of picking." ❖

THE MAPLES' ANNUAL GIFT

Long ago when the earth was new, according to Ojibwa legend, maple trees produced a sap that was as thick and sweet as syrup, and anyone who tapped the trees reaped an easy reward. But all-powerful Wenebojo, the trickster spirit, found this situation unacceptable. To ensure that humans did not take the earth's bounty for granted, he caused the sap of the maple trees to become thin and watery. Since that time, the Ojibwa people have had to work hard to obtain the maple sugar that nourishes them throughout the year.

For centuries the Indians of the Great Lakes have gathered at their family maple stand, often called the sugarbush, to celebrate the end of the long, hard winter season and to collect and render the sap of the sugar maple, which abounds in the forests of the region. The annual sugaring ritual takes place in the short interval as winter fades and spring begins. During that time, the warm days and freezing nights cause the sap stored in the roots of the trees to run beneath the bark, where it can be tapped. Since salt was not available to the Ojibwa, it was sugar that seasoned and preserved their food. Sugar cakes provided sustenance during the dangerous lean periods when there was little else to eat. And when the Ojibwa wished to thank their guiding spirits, the manitous, for their help, they frequently offered their most precious commodity—sugar.

Relatively few Indian families still work the sugarbushes of the woodlands around the lakes, and those that do tend to produce maple syrup for sale only. Here and on the pages that follow is a look at a more traditional sugar camp, run by Nick and Charlotte Hockings, an Ojibwa couple from Lac du Flambeau, Wisconsin. The Hockingses, with the help of their family and friends, produce not only syrup but also the cakes and granulated sugar that were made by their ancestors. They use no thermometers, hydrometers, or regulators common in modern operations to produce this sweet harvest—relying instead on their own muscle and the knowledge and observations passed down through untold generations.

Nick Hockings saws firewood amid the paraphernalia of his sugar camp on the Lac du Flambeau Ojibwa reservation. Only dead-wood is culled as fuel for the constant fires needed to process the sap.

Hockings lifts an offering of tobacco to a grandfather maple in the family sugarbush. Tobacco is traditionally offered as thanks to the spirits for the bounty that will be taken from the land.

Years of experience give Hockings a feel for which trees are likely to produce good sap and how to tap them. Once a tree is selected, a hole is bored into the trunk to the appropriate depth and angle (left) to accept a small spout that is then gently yet firmly hammered into the tree (above). Care must be taken not to split the wood or bend the spout.

TAPPING THE TREES

After setting the tap, Hockings hangs a bucket from the spout (above) to receive the sap. Drop by drop, the buckets fill with the slightly sweet "tree water" (right). During a good sap run, each bucket might fill up twice a day.

The sugar maker pushes a barrel on a sled through a late-season snowfall as he goes about the chore of collecting sap from the tree buckets. The buckets must be vigilantly checked and emptied lest they overflow and the precious fluid be wasted on the ground. Sap that is not immediately processed can be stored for a short time and boiled later.

Between sap runs, Hockings can usually be found stocking the woodpile. During sugaring season, huge amounts of deadwood must be cleared, gathered, cut, and split to feed the fires under the kettles. It is said that it takes the equivalent of a log the size of a man to cook one gallon of maple syrup.

BOILING THE SAP

Fresh sap is poured into a large iron trough in preparation for the first boil in the sugaring process (left). Maple sap contains only two to three percent sugar, so a steady fire is maintained underneath the trough in order to concentrate the liquid. When the sap is tasted and deemed sufficiently cooked, it is drawn off into buckets (below) and taken to the next cooking stage.

After the first boil, the thickened liquid is poured into a cauldron for further cooking. The steaming kettle has to be watched closely to ensure that the syrup does not burn or boil over.

Pure maple syrup (right) is the product of the second boil. The Ojibwa did not traditionally keep syrup on hand throughout the year, preferring the portability of the dry sugar products obtained through further cooking.

Hockings chops out a rough-hewed hook to hold the cooking pot over the fire during the final boil down to sugar (left and above). Many useful objects such as hooks, spoons, and bark cones for holding sugar cakes are crafted while the liquid slowly cooks.

The sugar maker casts a practiced eye on a nearly finished batch of sugar (left) and pours a sample onto a handful of snow for quick cooling (above). Split-second timing is required to get the mixture just right for making the sugar cakes. Overcooking causes the solution to granulate.

THE REWARDS OF HARD LABOR

Once the test sugar is cooled, its flavor and consistency tell Hockings if it is done (left). Once a batch is ready for caking, it must be poured quickly into the wooden squares and cone-shaped bark molds to harden (below). Any granulated remains, as shown in the pot below, can also be used.

A FEAST OF THANKS

A cleansing smoke sends the gratitude of the sugar makers to the heavens preceding the Migwetch Feast, an Ojibwa tradition hosted by Nick and Charlotte Hockings (at center) for the family and friends who helped out in the sugarbush. Their hard work was rewarded by the syrup, sugar cakes, and maple sugar to be enjoyed during the coming year (below).

ACKNOWLEDGMENTS

The editors wish to thank the following individuals and institutions for their valuable assistance in the preparation of this volume:

In Canada:
Quebec—Chris Kirby, Canadian Museum of Civilization, Hull; David Gidmark, Maniwaki.

In Denmark:
Copenhagen—Berete Due, National Museum.

In Germany:
Berlin—Peter Bolz, Staatliche Museen zu Berlin, Preussischer Kulturbesitz, Museum für Völkerkunde. Stuttgart—Ursula Didoni, Linden-Museum.

In the United States:
Indiana: South Bend—Greg Ballew, Henry Bush.
Iowa: Cedar Falls—Jack Minehart, Big Fork Canoe Trails.
Michigan: Dowagiac—Rae Daugherty.
Minnesota: Bemidji—Earl Nyholm, Bemidji State University. Minneapolis—Layne Kennedy. St. Paul—

Tracy Baker, Sherri Gebert Fuller, Minnesota Historical Society.
South Carolina: Aiken—Julie McCrum, Wooden Canoe Heritage Association.
Virginia: Newport News—R. Thomas Crew, Jr., The Mariners' Museum.
Wisconsin: Bayfield—Marvin DeFoe, Red Cliff Band of Lake Superior Chippewas. Lac du Flambeau—Charlotte Hockings, Nick Hockings, Wa Swa Goning Traditional Ojibwa Village, Lac du Flambeau Indian Reservation. Milwaukee—Susan Otto, Milwaukee Public Museum.

BIBLIOGRAPHY

BOOKS

Adney, Edwin Tappan, and Howard I. Chapelle, *The Bark Canoes and Skin Boats of North America.* Washington, D.C.: Smithsonian Institution, 1964.

America's Fascinating Indian Heritage. Pleasantville, New York: Reader's Digest Association, 1990.

Barnouw, Victor, *Wisconsin Chippewa Myths & Tales and Their Relation to Chippewa Life.* Madison: University of Wisconsin Press, 1977.

Benton-Banai, Edward, *The Mishomis Book: The Voice of the Ojibway.* St. Paul: Indian Country Press, 1979.

Berkhofer, Robert F., Jr., *Salvation and the Savage: An Analysis of Protestant Missions and American Indian Response, 1787-1862.* Lexington: University of Kentucky Press, 1965.

Blair, Emma Helen, ed., and transl., *The Indian Tribes of the Upper Mississippi Valley and Region of the Great Lakes.* Vol. 1. New York: Kraus Reprint, 1969 (reprint of 1911 edition).

Bonvillain, Nancy, *The Huron.* New York: Chelsea House Publishers, 1989.

Butterfield, C. W., *History of the Discovery of the Northwest by John Nicolet in 1634 with a Sketch of His Life.* Port Washington, New York: Kennikat Press, 1969.

Cleland, Charles E., *Rites of Conquest: The History and Culture of Michigan's Native Americans.* Ann Arbor: University of Michigan Press, 1992.

Clifton, James A., *The Potawatomi.* New York: Chelsea House Publishers, 1987.

Conway, Thor, and Julie Conway, *Spirits on Stone: The Agawa Pictographs.* San Luis Obispo, California: Heritage Discoveries, 1990.

Curtis, Natalie, ed., *The Indians' Book: An Offering by the American Indians of Indian Lore, Musical and Narrative, to Form a Record of the Songs and Legends of Their Race.* New York: Dover Publications, 1968.

Danziger, E. J., Jr., *The Chippewas of Lake Superior.* Norman: University of Oklahoma Press, 1979.

Densmore, Frances:
Chippewa Customs. St. Paul: Minnesota Historical Society Press, 1979.
Chippewa Music. Washington, D.C.: Government Printing Office, 1910.

Dewdney, Selwyn, *The Sacred Scrolls of the Southern Ojibway.* Toronto: University of Toronto Press, 1975.

Dewdney, Selwyn, and Kenneth E. Kidd, *Indian Rock Paintings of the Great Lakes.* Toronto: University of Toronto Press, 1962.

Eccles, W. J., *France in America.* East Lansing: Michigan State University Press, 1990.

Ewing, Douglas C., *Pleasing the Spirits: A Catalogue of a Collection of American Indian Art.* New York: Ghylen Press, 1982.

Feest, Christian F., *Native Arts of North America.* London: Thames and Hudson, 1992.

Gemming, Elizabeth, *Maple Harvest: The Story of Maple Sugaring.* New York: Coward, McCann & Geoghegan, 1976.

Gidmark, David, *Birchbark Canoe: The Story of an Apprenticeship with the Indians.* Burnstown, Ontario: General Store Publishing House, 1989.

Gilman, Carolyn, *Where Two Worlds Meet: The Great Lakes Fur Trade.* St. Paul: Minnesota Historical Society Press, 1982.

Graymont, Barbara, *The Iroquois.* New York: Chelsea House Publishers, 1988.

Grim, John A., *The Shaman: Patterns of Religious Healing among the Ojibway Indians.* Norman: University of Oklahoma Press, 1983.

Henry, Alexander, *Travels and Adventures in Canada and the Indian Territories.* New York: Garland Publishing, 1976.

Hickerson, Harold, *The Chippewa and Their Neighbors: A Study in Ethnohistory.* Prospect Heights, Illinois: Waveland Press, 1988.

Hirschfelder, Arlene, and Paulette Molin, *The Encyclopedia of Native American Religions: An Introduction.* New York: Facts On File, 1992.

Hoffman, W. J., *The Mide'wiwin or "Grand Medicine Society" of the Ojibwa.* Washington, D.C.: Government Printing Office, 1891.

Jenness, Diamond, *The Ojibwa Indians of Parry Island, Their Social and Religious Life.* Ottawa: Canada Department of Mines, National Museum of Canada, 1935.

Johnston, Basil, *Ojibway Ceremonies.* Toronto: McClelland & Stewart, 1982.

Jones, William, *Ojibwa Texts.* Vol. 7, Part 1. Ed. by Truman Michelson. Leyden, Netherlands: E. J. Brill, 1917.

Keesing, Felix M., *The Menomini Indians of Wisconsin.* New York: Johnson Reprint, 1971 (reprint of 1939 edition).

Kinietz, W. Vernon, *The Indians of the Western Great Lakes: 1615-1760.* Ann Arbor: University of Michigan Press, 1990.

Kohl, Johann Georg, *Kitchi-Gami: Life among the Lake Superior Ojibway.* Transl. by Lascelles Wraxall. St. Paul: Minnesota Historical Society Press, 1985.

Landes, Ruth, *The Ojibwa Woman.* New York: Columbia University Press, 1938.

Lyford, Carrie A., *The Crafts of the Ojibwa (Chippewa).* Phoenix: Office of Indian Affairs, 1943.

McCracken, Harold, *George Catlin and the Old Frontier.* New York: Dial Press, 1959.

McPhee, John, *The Survival of the Bark Canoe.* New York: Farrar, Straus and Giroux, 1975.

Nabokov, Peter, and Robert Easton, *Native American Architecture.* New York: Oxford University Press, 1989.

Nearing, Helen, and Scott Nearing, *The Maple Sugar Book.* New York: Galahad Books, 1970.

Ourada, Patricia K., *The Menominee.* New York: Chelsea House Publishers, 1990.

Penney, David W., ed., *Art of the American Indian Frontier: The Chandler-Pohrt Collection.* Seattle: University of Washington Press, 1992.

Phillips, Ruth B., *Patterns of Power: The Jasper Grant Collection and Great Lakes Indian Art of the Early Nineteenth Century.* Kleinburg, Ontario: The McMichael Canadian Collection, 1984.

Radin, Paul, *The Winnebago Tribe.* Lincoln: University of Nebraska Press, 1970.

Ritzenthaler, Robert E., *Building a Chippewa Indian Birchbark Canoe.* Milwaukee: Milwaukee Public Museum, 1984.

Ritzenthaler, Robert E., and Pat Ritzenthaler, *The Woodland Indians of the Western Great Lakes.* Prospect Heights, Illinois: Waveland Press, 1983.

Roberts, Kenneth G., and Philip Shackleton, *The Canoe: Craft from Panama to the Arctic.* Camden, Maine: International Marine Publishing, 1983.

Schoolcraft, Henry R., *Narrative Journal of Travels through the Northwestern Regions of the United States Extending from Detroit through the Great Chain of American Lakes to the Sources of the Mississippi River in the Year 1820.* Ed. by Mentor L. Williams. East Lansing: Michigan State College Press, 1953.

Tanner, Helen Hornbeck, *The Ojibwa.* New York: Chelsea House Publishers, 1992.

Tanner, Helen Hornbeck, ed., *Atlas of Great Lakes Indian History.* Norman: University of Oklahoma Press, 1987.

Thompson, Stith, *Tales of the North American Indians.* Bloomington: Indiana University Press, 1966.

Thwaites, Reuben Gold, ed., *New Voyages to North-America by the Baron de Lahontan.* Vol. 1. New York: Burt Franklin, 1970 (reprint of 1905 edition).

Torrence, Gaylord, and Robert Hobbs, *Art of the Red Earth People: The Mesquakie of Iowa.* Seattle: University of Washington Press, 1989.

Trigger, Bruce G., ed., *Northeast.* Vol. 15 of *Handbook of North American Indians.* Washington, D.C.: Smithsonian Institution, 1978.

Vecsey, Christopher, *Traditional Ojibwa Religion and Its Historical Changes.* Philadelphia: American Philosophical Society, 1983.

Vennum, Thomas, Jr., *Wild Rice and the Ojibway People.* St. Paul: Minnesota Historical Society Press, 1988.

Viola, Herman J., *The Indian Legacy of Charles Bird King.* Washington, D.C.: Smithsonian Institution Press, 1976.

Vizenor, Gerald, *The People Named the Chippewa: Narrative Histories.* Minneapolis: University of Minnesota Press, 1984.

Vizenor, Gerald, ed., *Summer in the Spring: Anishinaabe Lyric Poems and Stories.* Norman: University of Oklahoma Press, 1993.

Warren, William W., *History of the Ojibway People.* St. Paul: Minnesota Historical Society Press, 1984.

PERIODICALS

Barnouw, Victor:
"A Chippewa Mide Priest's Description of the Medicine Dance." *The Wisconsin Archeologist,* December 1960.

"Reminiscences of a Chippewa Mide Priest." *The Wisconsin Archeologist,* December 1954.

Black, A. K., "Shaking the Wigwam: A Vivid Description of Indian Occult Practices which Proves that Black Magic is Not Restricted to the Congo." *The Beaver,* December 1934.

Kolb, Richard K., "Last Stand at Leech Lake." *Army,* June 1987.

Luoma, Jon R., "Rare Species and Ecosystems Abundant in Great Lakes Region." *The New York Times,* February 22, 1994.

Minehart, Jack, "The Legacy of William Hafeman." *Canoe,* July 1981.

National Geographic Society:
"Land Between the Waters." *National Geographic Magazine,* August 1973.

"The Making of America: Great Lakes." *National Geographic Magazine,* July 1987.

Roddis, Louis H., "The Last Indian Uprising in the United States." *Minnesota History Bulletin,* February 1920.

Stephens, Peter J., "Long Live the Bark Canoe." *Wood Magazine,* April 1990.

Tanner, Helen Hornbeck, "The Career of Joseph La France, *Coureur de Bois* in the Upper Great Lakes." *The Fur Trade Revisited: Selected Papers of the Sixth North American Fur Trade Conference, Mackinac Island, Michigan, 1991.* Ed. by Jennifer S. H. Brown, W. J. Eccles, and Donald P. Heldman. East Lansing: Michigan State University Press, 1994.

Vennum, Thomas, Jr., "Ojibwa Origin-Migration Songs of the Mitewiwin." *Journal of American Folklore,* July-September 1978.

Wilcox, U. Vincent, "The Museum of the American Indian." *American Indian Art Magazine,* Spring 1978.

OTHER PUBLICATIONS

The Art of the Great Lakes Indians. Flint, Michigan: Flint Institute of Arts, 1973.

Coe, Ralph T., *Sacred Circles: Two Thousand Years of North American Indian Art.* Catalog. Kansas City, Missouri: Nelson Gallery of Art-Atkins Museum of Fine Arts, 1977.

Cooke, Sarah E., and Rachel B. Ramadhyani, *Indians and a Changing Frontier: The Art of George Winter.* Catalog. Indianapolis: Indiana Historical Society, 1993.

Kegg, Maude, *Gabekanaansing/at the End of the Trail: Memories of Chippewa Childhood in Minnesota with Texts in Ojibwe and English.* Ed. by John Nichols. Occasional Publications in Anthropology Linguistics Series No. 4. Greeley: Museum of Anthropology, University of Northern Colorado, 1978.

Tanner, John, *An Indian Captivity (1789-1822): John Tanner's Narrative of His Captivity among the Ottawa and Ojibwa Indians.* Paper. Ed. by Edwin James. Parts 1 and 2. San Francisco: California State Library, 1940.

PICTURE CREDITS

68: Marvin De Foe; Jack Minehart. **69:** Art by Wood, Ronsaville, Harlin, Inc. **70, 71:** From the Williams/Daugherty Collection, contributed by Rae Daugherty; Marvin De Foe—art by Wood, Ronsaville, Harlin, Inc. **72, 73:** Jack Minehart; Marvin De Foe—art by Wood, Ronsaville, Harlin, Inc. **74:** Jack Minehart—art by Wood, Ronsaville, Harlin, Inc. **75:** David Gidmark. **76:** Milwaukee Public Museum. **78:** Minnesota Historical Society. **80:** © The Detroit Institute of Arts, Founders Society Purchase with funds from Flint Ink Corporation. Robert Hensleigh, photographer. **81:** Milwaukee Public Museum, neg. no. 5951. **82, 83:** Craig Blacklock/Blacklock Nature Photography, Moose Lake, Minn. **85:** Neg. no. 316346, photo by J. K. Dixon, courtesy Department of Library Services, American Museum of Natural History. **87:** © The Detroit Institute of Arts, Founders Society Purchase. **88:** NAA, Smithsonian Institution, neg. no. 43551-A. **90, 91:** Minnesota Historical Society; Henry B. Beville, courtesy Smithsonian Institution. **92:** Smithsonian Institution, catalog no. 88-11738. **94, 95:** Minnesota Historical Society. **96, 97:** © The Detroit Institute of Arts, Founders Society Purchase—© The Detroit Institute of Arts, Founders Society Purchase. Robert Hensleigh, photographer; Milwaukee Public Museum, neg. no. 29. **98:** Canadian Museum of Civilization, Hull, neg. no. 36683. **99:** Milwaukee Public Museum. **100:** NAA, Smithsonian Institution, neg. no. 8392. **101:** Minnesota Historical Society. **102:** Museum für Völkerkunde, Vienna, Austria. **103:** NAA, Smithsonian Institution, neg. no. 54837. **104:** NAA, Smithsonian Institution, neg. no. 504. **106, 107:** Tippecanoe County Historical Association, Lafayette, Ind., gift of Mrs. Cable G. Ball. **108, 109:** St. Louis County Historical Society. **110:** NAA, Smithsonian Institution, neg. no. 476-A-22—Canadian Museum of Civilization, Hull, neg. no. A75-636. **111:** NAA, Smithsonian Institution, neg. no. 476-A-3. **112:** NAA, Smithsonian Institution, neg. no. 476-A-14—copyright British Museum, London. **113:** NAA, Smithsonian Institution, neg. no. 476-A-6. **114:** NAA, Smithsonian Institution, neg. no. 476-A-21. **115:** NAA, Smithsonian Institution, neg. no. 476-A-8; copyright British Museum, London. **116:** NAA, Smithsonian Institution, neg. no. 476-A-9. **117:** NAA, Smithsonian Institution, neg. no. 476-A-20—Smithsonian Institution, catalog no. 80-16639. **118, 119:** Glenbow Museum; neg. no. 316343, photo by C. M. Dixon, courtesy Department of Library Services, American Museum of Natural History. **120:** Museum Collections, Minnesota Historical Society. **121:** Courtesy Richard Manoogian Collection. © Robert Hensleigh, photographer, DIA; courtesy Cranbrook Institute of Science, CIS 3690. © Robert Hensleigh, photographer, DIA; courtesy Cranbrook Institute of Science, CIS 2322. © Robert Hensleigh, photographer, DIA. **122, 123:** Courtesy Cranbrook Institute of Science, CIS 2135. © Robert Hensleigh, photographer, DIA—photo by Carmelo Guadagno, courtesy National Museum of the American Indian, Smithsonian Institution, catalog no. 19/6346; National Museum of Ireland, Dublin; Canadian Museum of Civilization, Hull, neg. no. 94-37.674; copyright British Museum, London. **124, 125:** © The Detroit Institute of Arts, Founders Society Purchase (3)—National Museum of Ireland, Dublin. **126:** © The Detroit Institute of Arts, Founders Society Purchase (2)—Logan Museum of Anthropology, Beloit College, The Albert Green Heath Collection, photo by John S. Latimer. **127:** © The Detroit Institute of Arts, Founders Society Purchase with funds from the Flint Ink Corporation. **128:** Courtesy Detroit Historical Museum. © Robert Hensleigh, photographer, DIA; courtesy Detroit Historical Museum. © Dirk Bakker, photographer, DIA.

129: Courtesy Potawatomi Tribal Administration and the Field Museum. © Dirk Bakker, photographer, DIA. **130:** NAA, Smithsonian Institution, neg. no. 3793-B. **132:** Hudson's Bay Company Archives, Provincial Archives of Manitoba—Bibliothèque Nationale de France, Paris. **134:** Jean-Loup Charmet, Paris; Musée de l'Homme, photo by Cl. M. Delaplanche. **135:** National Archives of Canada, Ottawa, neg. no. C17653. **136, 137:** Bibliothèque Nationale de France, Paris. **139:** Archives Nationales, Paris. **140, 141:** National Gallery of Canada, Ottawa. **143:** Map by Maryland CartoGraphics, Inc. **144, 145:** Painting by William Armstrong, National Archives of Canada, Ottawa, neg. no. C-19041. **146, 147:** National Archives of Canada, Ottawa, neg. no. 3/3 A1100/1777; Museum Collections, Minnesota Historical Society (2). **148, 149:** Museum Collections, Minnesota Historical Society. **150:** Bibliothèque Nationale de France, Paris. **151:** Courtesy Richard and Marion Pohrt. © Robert Hensleigh, photographer. **152:** The Newberry Library—painting by Joshua Jebb, National Archives of Canada, Ottawa, neg. no. C-114384. **154, 155:** State Historical Society of Wisconsin. **157:** Library of Congress, USZ262-14142—Detroit Public Library. **160:** Tippecanoe County Historical Association, Lafayette, Ind., gift of Mrs. Cable G. Ball. **163:** NAA, Smithsonian Institution, neg. no. 45479-F. **164:** NAA, Smithsonian Institution, neg. no. 56520. **165:** NAA, Smithsonian Institution, neg. no. 3793-A. **166:** NAA, Smithsonian Institution, neg. no. 596-D-8. **167:** NAA, Smithsonian Institution, neg. no. 616-W-1—Milwaukee Public Museum. **168:** NAA, Smithsonian Institution, neg. no. 741A. **169:** Milwaukee Public Museum, neg. no. 35-17-20; NAA, Smithsonian Institution, neg. no. 727-D-10-C. **170:** National Archives. **173:** Minnesota Historical Society. **174-185:** Charlotte Hockings, Lac du Flambeau, Wis.

INDEX